Revised

Ne

Childrens Illustrated History

O.L. Henderson
Richard Ward

CLASS 3

OXFORD
UNIVERSITY PRESS

OXFORD
UNIVERSITY PRESS

Oxford University Press is a department of the University of Oxford. It furthers the University's objective of excellence in research, scholarship, and education by publishing worldwide. Oxford is a registered trade mark of Oxford University Press in the UK and in certain other countries.

Published in India by
Oxford University Press
YMCA Library Building, 1 Jai Singh Road, New Delhi 110001, India

First published as *A Children's Illustrated History*, 1977
Revised as *New Children's Illustrated History*, 1997
Third edition 2007
21st impression 2017

ISBN-13: 978-0-19-568384-4
ISBN-10: 0-19-568384-6

Typeset in Aldine BT 401
by Bukprint, Delhi
Printed in India by Repro India Ltd., Navi Mumbai

Illustrations by Kallol Majumder

Preface

There is general agreement among historians and history teachers in favour of creating a background of world history before children are introduced to the history of their own country. This gives students a sense of continuity when they study the history of their own people. This book is the first in a series of three books on world history for the Junior School. This preliminary course aims at introducing the child to the various phases of historical development beginning with the earliest civilizations.

This new edition has been thoroughly revised taking into account the feedback given by teachers. Many new elements have been added. The concept of **timelines** gives the children an idea of the time frame and brings events into perspective. Most of the chapters now have **maps** to give the children a sense of the geographical locations. **New topics and chapters** have been included to make it more current and up-to-date. **Did you knows** add interest. The activity section includes interactive and exciting **things to do** which will develop the children's interest in history.

This book for Class 3 begins with an introduction to history and concludes with the death of Julius Caesar. Class 4 begins with a chapter on Jesus Christ and takes the child up to the eighteenth century. In Class 5 the child is introduced to the American War of Independence and ends with the achievements of Nelson Mandela. The three books take the child from the past to the present. Each chapter is in the form of a story or a simple narrative told interestingly. Both biographical and culture-epoch methods have been used. The heroes of war and peace find their place in the former method while the latter approach highlights important historical events and processes. The chapters are arranged chronologically with timelines given at the beginning. The children are made aware of the development of writing, town planning, states, empires and religions. At all times the level of understanding displayed by the children in that particular age-group has been kept in mind.

The photographs and illustrations have been chosen, as far as possible, from contemporary or traditional sources rather than from fanciful reconstruction. Children are introduced to sources of history when they try to relate these materials to the findings of historians. The exercises reinforce learning. Word-notes at the beginning of each chapter draw attention to new ideas or concepts introduced in the chapter as well as to words that might be unfamiliar to the child.

Contents

Prehistory — The period for which there are no written records

History — The period for which there are written records

History

—A record of the past

History is a written record of events that happened in the past. It tells us about the people who lived in earlier times.

It tells us what these people did every day, how they grew their food, how they became rich or poor, how they lived, how they built great cities, how they fought one another and how they helped one another.

History tells us about the past

Words to remember

excavate : take out things that have been buried in the ground.
conquered : took possession of (land, etc.) by force.
explorers : people who travel to different places and countries to learn more about them.
monuments : old buildings and statues that remind people about things, people or events of the past.
events : things that happen.
papyrus : paper made from a type of grass growing on the banks of the Nile.

It also tells us about the lives of great people. It tells us where they lived and what they did. Some were great rulers. Others fought battles and became famous **conquerors**. Some of them were famous teachers. They taught people how to lead good lives. There are many others about whom we study in history books—writers and **explorers**, scientists, artists, musicians and thinkers. We can learn a lot from the lives of these great people.

Why do we learn history? First, because it is interesting. People want to know what happened in the past. It is exciting to read about the past. History also helps us to understand the world we live in today. We can learn from the mistakes which people made in the past.

Did you know?

Herodotus, a Greek writer is known as the Father of History. He is famous for writing *The Histories*, a collection of stories about places and people.

Like we said earlier, history is a written record. Many thousands of years ago, people did not have paper. So, what did they write on? Some people wrote on stones; and even on the **bark** of trees. People also wrote on **papyrus**, which was made from the thick grass-like plant which grows near some rivers and lakes. Some people wrote on **metal plates** of copper and silver.

Ancient writing on papyrus

Writing on bark

Stone inscription

Paper was invented in China. From there it spread to other parts of the world and came to be commonly used for writing. As people travelled, and went from one country to another, they told each other about these forms of writing.

How was writing invented? Given below are some pictures. They tell us a little about how the letters came from pictures of things.

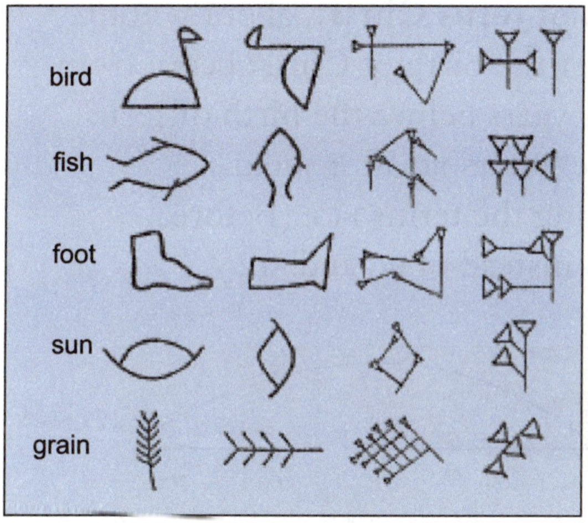

Ancient writings from Mesopotamia

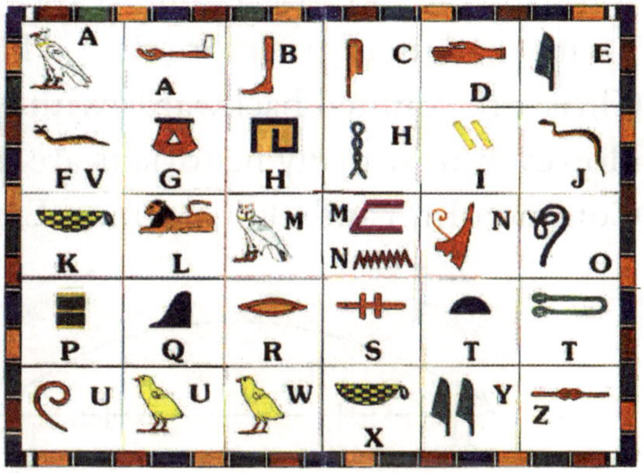

Ancient writings of Egypt

Although most of the history we know comes to us from books, we learn history in other ways, too. We learn history from buildings and **monuments**; some people dig below the ground to find old cities that have been buried there. These people are known as **archaeologists**. They learn a lot about the people who lived in the cities by looking carefully at the things they **excavate**. The study of things, buildings and

Archaeologists at work

monuments that people have left behind is known as **archaeology**.

History tells us about the past. Therefore, dates of events are quite important because they give us an idea of when events took place. When you read history books you will often find the letters BC and AD after or before dates. For example, Ashoka died in 232 BC; Akbar was born in AD 1556. These letters stand for *Before Christ* and *Anno Domini* which in Latin means 'in the year of our Lord'. As you can see, all these dates are counted from the birth of **Jesus Christ**, about whom you will read in Class 4. The years after the birth of Christ begin from 1 with the letters AD before them. The years before the birth of Jesus Christ are counted backwards with the letters BC after them. However, now many historians are using the terms BCE (Before Common Era) and CE (Common Era) instead of BC and AD.

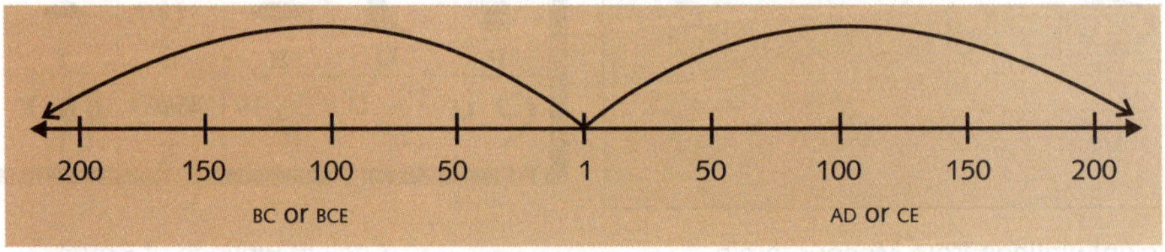

A **timeline** helps us to understand when certain historical events took place. It is a line of dates in which all the dates related to a certain event or person are arranged in the right order. For example, suppose you were born in 1997 then your timeline would be like this:

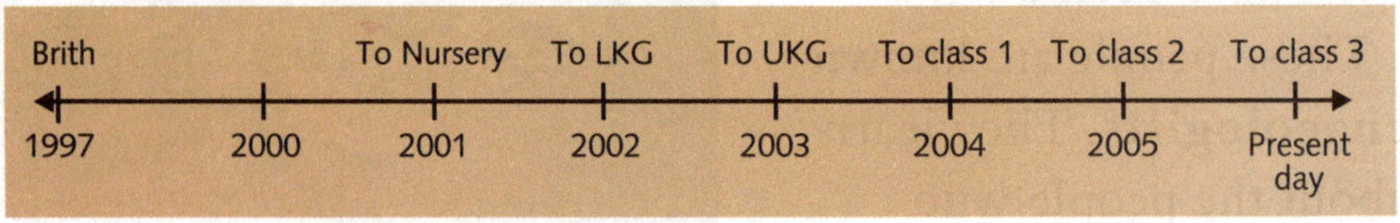

Every chapter is introduced with a timeline so that you can understand how long ago the event took place.

Exercises

1. **Answer the following.**
   (a) Write down the names of six stories which you have read in class.
   (b) Write down the names of six stories you have heard, either from your teacher or from your parents.
   (c) What does history tell us?
   (d) What do the words BC and AD stand for?
   (e) What is archaeology?

2. **Fill in the blanks.**
   (a) We learn history because it is ....
   (b) People in ancient times sometimes wrote on.................... made of reeds.
   (c) We can learn from other people's ....
   (d) We learn history from buildings and ....

3. **Say whether the following are True or False.**
   (a) History tells us only about things which great people did.
   (b) Paper was invented in India.
   (c) History helps us to understand the world we live in today.
   (d) All our dates are counted from the birth of Jesus Christ.

Things to do

1. **For your scrapbook!**
   Make a scrapbook and keep filling it up as you complete the chapter. Try to find as many letters as you can from different

alphabets or scripts. For example:
The English Alphabet a b c d
Devnagari ....
Tamil ....
Your mother tongue..
Cut out samples from magazines, newspapers or books in different languages.

2. **Group activity.**
Make five to six groups. Each group can paint a clay pot. Then put it in a bag and break it. Once all the pots are broken, mix the pieces and bury them. Now dig them out, match them and put them back together.

3. **Shoebox archaeology.**
This activity helps students to understand how historians and archaeologists uncover clues to interpret our past.

You need: a shoebox; personal items such as coins, shells, bottles, dishes, ornaments and toys; things that belonged to or remind you of your grandparents, your parents, and your own things; soil; spoon and paintbrush.

Method: Fill the shoebox in the following order:
A thin layer of soil; some things relating to grandparents; a thin layer of soil; some things relating to your parents; a thin layer of soil; some of your personal possessions or photos; top with another thin layer of soil.

Number each shoebox. Distribute the boxes, making sure no student receives the one he or she assembled. Now 'excavate' the boxes. Note the order in which the things are uncovered and think about what they reveal about the personality and family history of the person whose box it is. At the end, try and guess who put the box together.

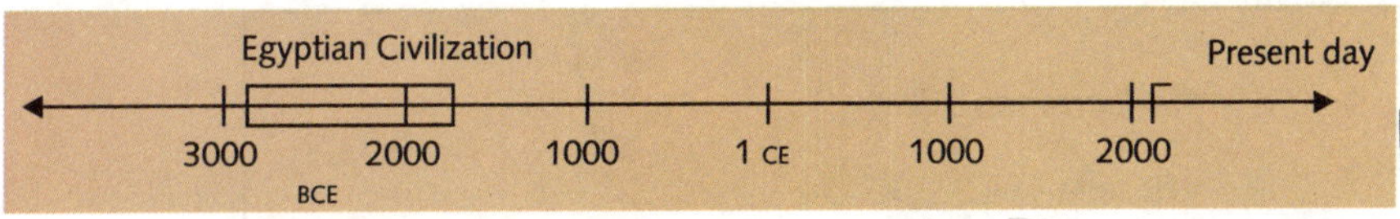

Egypt
—The land of the Pharaohs

Egypt is a country far away from India, in the continent of Africa. It is not a very big country but it has a great river flowing through it called the Nile. The Nile starts in the middle of Africa and flows through Egypt into the Mediterranean Sea. As it flows it carries fertile soil with it. Most of Egypt is desert. The land on either side of the river is good for growing crops, because each year the Nile brings it new soil. The Nile gives new life to the people of Egypt. It provides them with water for drinking, for their animals and for their fields. People can move about faster in their boats along the Nile.

Words to remember

Pharaoh : the name given to the Egyptian king.

pyramid : the stone tomb or building in which the Pharaoh's body was placed after his death.

embalm : to preserve a dead body from decay by covering it with spices or chemicals.

mummies : dead bodies that were embalmed to be kept fresh for a long time.

coffin : a box made out of wood or stone or metal in which the dead body is placed.

slaves : people who were taken as prisoners from countries that had been conquered and made to do hard work.

captured : taken prisoner.

Thousands of years ago there were many wandering tribes in Egypt.

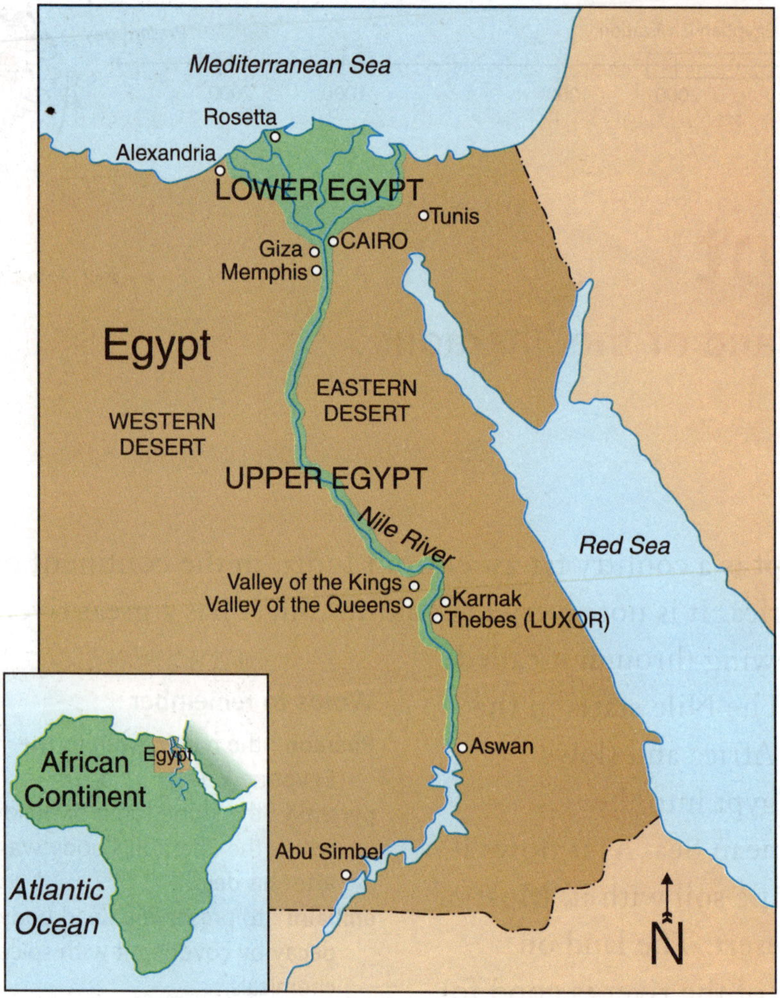

These people did not live in one place but went from place to place with their camels and donkeys in search of food. At some point (we do not know when) they found out that if they sow seeds in the ground plants would come up. They also found that if they sow seeds in the rich soil which came

Did you know?

We have come to know a lot about the Egyptians because we have been able to read their writing. The ancient Egyptians used a special kind of picture-writing called hieroglyphics.

down with the river Nile, crops would grow very well indeed. But if you sow seeds you have to wait for some months before the crops come up. This meant that the people who sowed the seeds had to stay in one place for a long time. They could not wander about as they had done before. As they wanted to stay in one place, they built houses for themselves. More and more people built houses, and villages grew up. Slowly people learnt to build better houses out of stone and bricks, and then they began to build cities.

A painting showing farming in Egypt

The Egyptians became rich and happy. They discovered many things. They learnt how to build houses with stone and baked bricks, they learnt to write on papyrus and also how to make cloth.

They thought that the powerful sun was a god. They called the sun Ra and worshipped him. They built fine temples to the sun god and to other gods whom they worshipped. As they grew good crops of corn they were able to trade with other countries. They used gold and silver which they got from other countries in exchange for their corn for building the temples. They led a peaceful and settled life.

A painting,inside one of the pyramids showing the Egyptian sun god

Some men became richer and stronger than others, and soon some of these rich and strong men became kings. The Egyptians believed that their kings, whom they called **Pharaohs**, were children of the sun god. They thought that when people died they would go to another world. So when people died they put the dead bodies in tombs along with all their belongings, which they would need in the next world.

A wall painting showing a Pharaoh

When Pharaohs died, the Egyptians built huge tombs or **pyramids** made of stone. These pyramids were very beautifully made by skilled craftspeople. There were no building stones in Egypt and so stones for the pyramids had to be dragged from many miles away. All the hard work was done by **slaves**. These slaves were men whom the Egyptians had **captured** in battles with other countries. The slaves had to work very hard. They had to walk many miles, dragging the heavy stones across the desert on rollers. Each team of slaves had an Egyptian with a whip behind them, and if any slave did not work hard enough he was whipped cruelly. Some pyramids took many years to build. In each pyramid there was a secret passageway. When the pyramid was ready the dead body was **embalmed**, but we do not know exactly how they did it.

The Great Pyramid at Giza

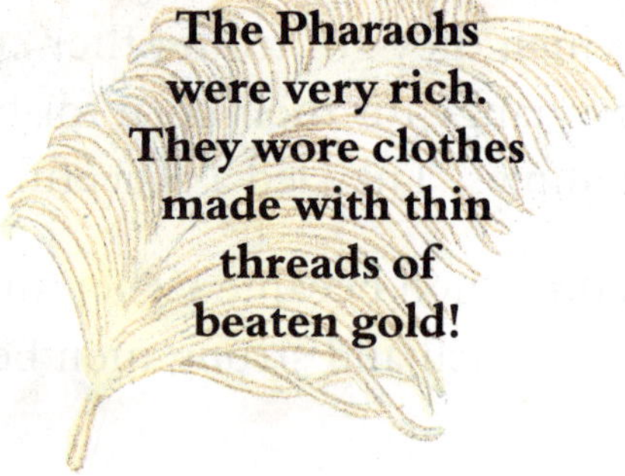

Did you know?

The Pharaohs were very rich. They wore clothes made with thin threads of beaten gold!

These bodies were then called **mummies**. The mummy was then carried down through the secret passage and put into the tomb. Along with it were buried things that the Egyptians believed the dead person would require on his journey to the other world. When all this had been done the passage was closed. Then the men who had built it were killed, so that no one could find the secret passage.

The Sphinx

The tallest pyramid is the Great Pyramid of Khufu. It is at Giza along with two smaller pyramids. Another very interesting monument is the Sphinx. It has the head of a man with the body of a lion. It has become famous as a symbol of the ancient Egyptian civilization.

One of the most important Pharaohs in Egypt was called Akhenaten. He had a very beautiful wife called Nefertiti. Akhenaten lived nearly

Nefertiti

Akhenaten

Mask of Tutankhamen

3,500 years ago. When he died his half-brother Tutankhamen became king in his place, Tutankhamen was only nine years old when he became king and he died at the age of 18. He was buried with all his treasures in a small tomb.

In 1922 a man called Howard Carter opened the tomb to find out what was inside. The body of Tutankhamen was still there in a beautiful gold **coffin**. This coffin was inside two more coffins. By the side of the coffins there was some food and oil. There were also the king's clothes and jewels. There were even some toys and walking sticks and a bunch of flowers. The flowers had still kept their shape even after 3,500 years. The things that were found in Tutankhamen's tomb are now in a museum in Cairo.

Howard Carter

The gold coffin

Exercises

1. Answer the following.

(a) How has the river Nile helped Egypt?

(b) What were the different things the Egyptians learnt to do?

(c) How were the slaves treated?

(d) Why did the Egyptians put all the belongings of the dead person beside him in his tomb?

(e) Who was Howard Carter?

(f) What was found inside Tutankhamen's coffin?

2. Fill in the blanks.

(a) The river .... flows through Egypt and carries fertile soil with it.

(b) The Egyptians worshipped ...., the sun god.

(c) In each pyramid there was a .... passage-way. The men who had built it were ....

(d) There were no building .... in Egypt and so they had to be .... from miles away.

(e) The dead bodies which the Egyptians embalmed were called ....

(f) The Great Pyramid is at ....

3. Match the following.

(a) Akhenaten	Howard Carter
(b) Tutankhamen	Nefertiti
(c) Sun god	Giza
(d) Great Pyramid	Ra

Things to do

1. **Be an artist!**
   Make a clay model of a pyramid or draw a picture of a pyramid.
2. **Solve the puzzle.**
   Complete the puzzle with the help of the clues given.

Across

2. A great river
3. The Egyptian king
5. Tombs
7. Groups of people
8. A crop the Egyptians grew

Down

1. Embalmed bodies of the pharaohs
2. The wife of Akhenaten
4. Egypt is in this continent
5. A kind of grass
6. The sun god

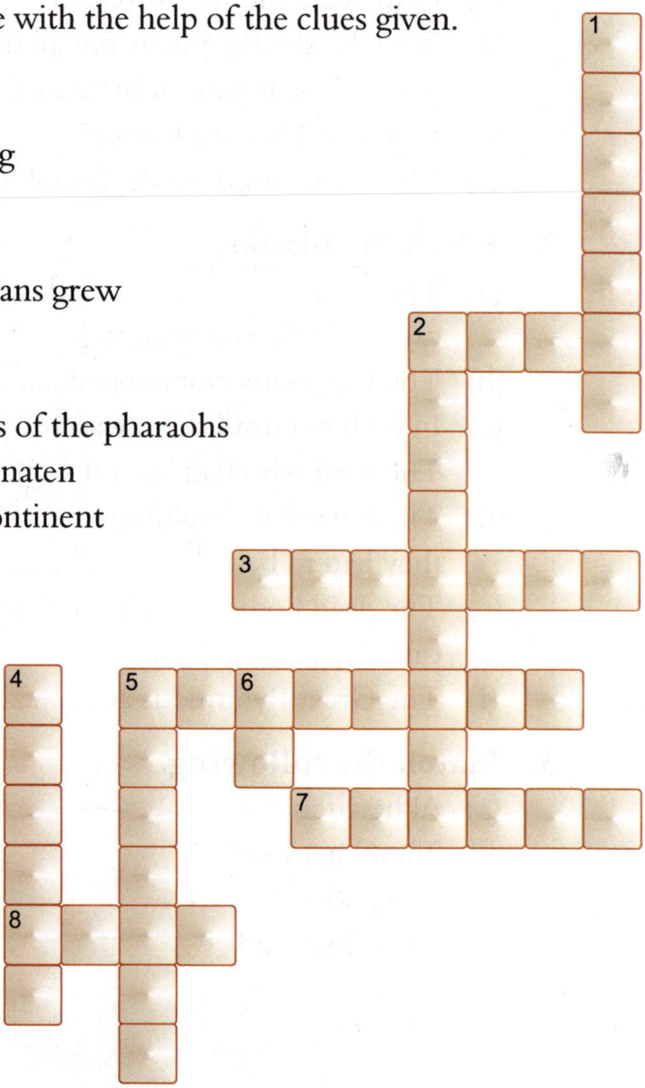

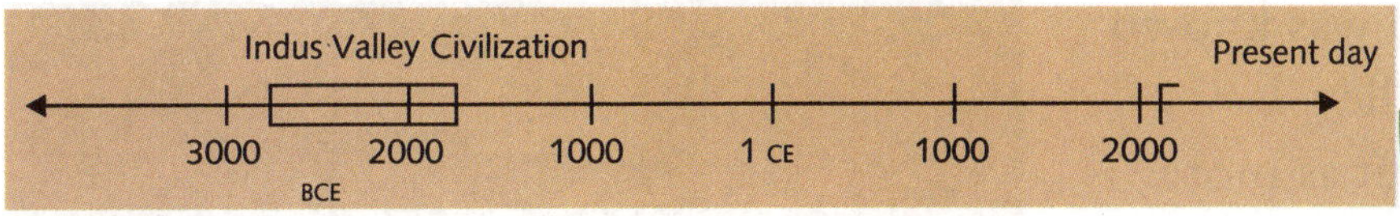

The Indus Valley

—A great Indian civilization

Thousands of years ago, a great civilization flourished near the river Indus. Among the cities that the people built, the two most famous were at Mohenjo Daro and Harappa. Everyone forgot about them, and thousands of years went by. The great cities of Mohenjo Daro and Harappa lay covered with sand. It was only in 1856, three thousand years later, when some men were building a railway line between Karachi and Lahore, that they came across some bricks lying near a mound. These bricks were so good that they used them for the railway tracks. They did not know that the bricks had been made by the stone masons of Harappa more than 3,000 years ago!

Later, in 1922, people began to dig the area called Mohenjo Daro, the mound of the dead—for that is what it means—and found out many wonderful things about the people of the Indus Valley.

When these cities were first discovered,

Words to remember

seals : pieces made of metal or clay or other materials with designs on them.

ruins : the remains of old cities and buildings.

granary : a place where grain is stored.

weapons : things used in fighting.

fortified : made strong so that it cannot be easily taken by the enemy.

this civilization was known as the Indus Valley Civilization. But as more and more cities were found in places away from the Indus River, historians named it the Harappan Civilization.

The ruins of Mohenjo Daro

Seals

We have come to know many things about the people of Egypt because we can read what they wrote. The people of Harappa and Mohenjo Daro wrote on **seals**. But we have not yet been able to read what is written on these seals. Many other things have been discovered about these people who lived more than 3,600 years ago, from the **ruins** of these two great cities.

Both cities were built on the same plan. Houses were built of burnt bricks, with square courtyards, bathrooms and very good drains to carry the dirty water away. The roads were straight and broad. The most important building that has been found at Mohenjo Daro is the great bath-house.

The Great Bath

It had a swimming pool, changing-rooms and bathrooms, and one could even take a cold shower if one wanted to! To the west of the great bath-house was a large **granary**. All the grain was stored there. Some of it was sent to other countries, and the people of the Indus Valley got other things in exchange.

Granaries

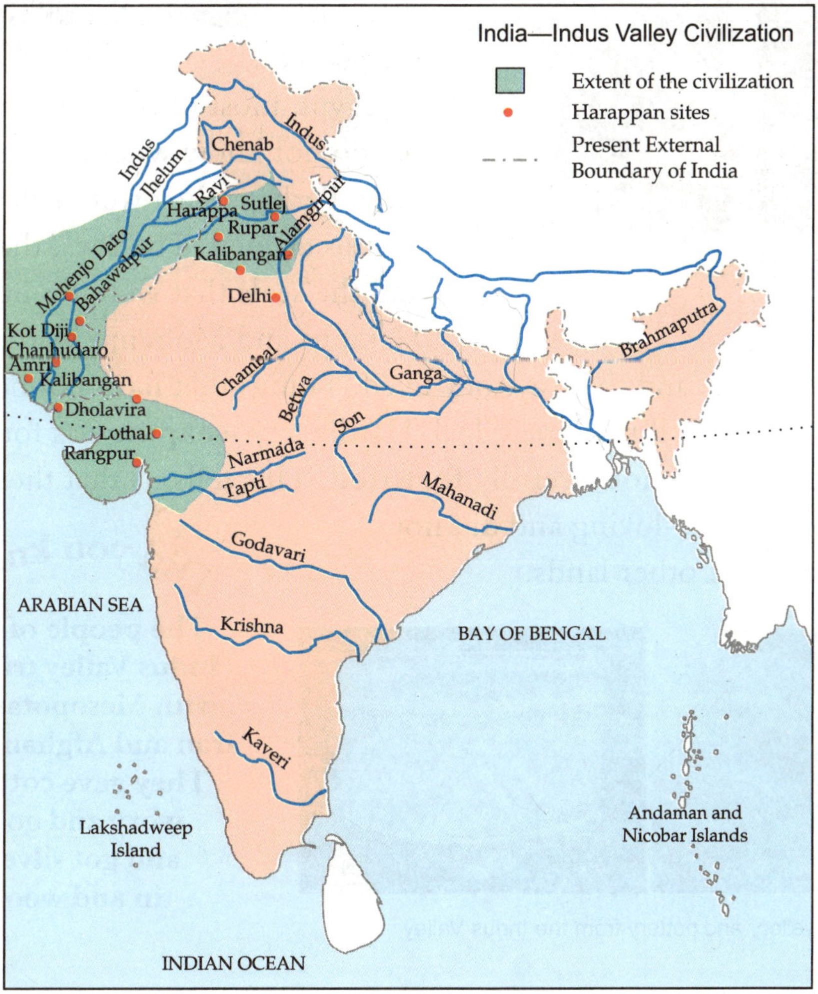

We can find out many things about the people from the statues that have been found at these **ruins**. The men wore robes which left one shoulder bare and the women kept long hair. The children had beautiful toys—animals which could nod their heads. The seals tell us about the gods and goddesses that the Indus Valley people worshipped. We also come to know from

The priest king

these seals that, like the people

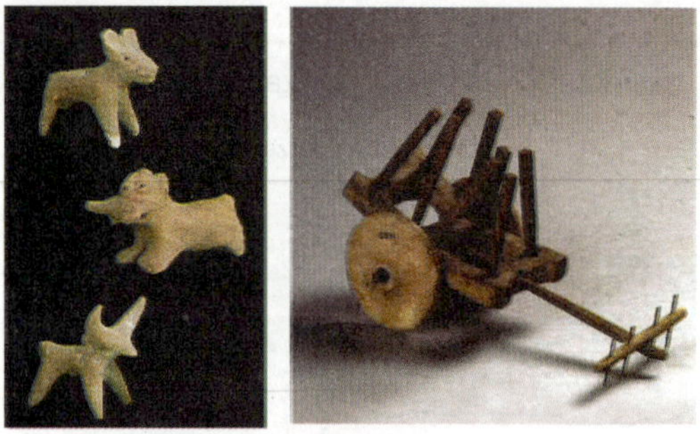

Toys

of Egypt, most of them grew crops. We do not know whether they had a king. Perhaps they were ruled by groups of men. The toys, the statues and the seals that were found at Harappa and Mohenjo Daro tell us about the people and the way they lived. Things that have not been found there also tell us a great deal. Hardly any **weapon** was found and the cities were not carefully **fortified**. This tells us that these people were peace-loving and did not wish to conquer other lands.

Jewellery and pottery from the Indus Valley

Did you know?

The people of the Indus Valley traded with Mesopotamia, Iran and Afghanistan. They gave cotton, ivory and gold and got silver, tin and wool.

What happened to these very clever Indus Valley people? No one knows for certain. Some think that the Great Indian Desert slowly destroyed their land and drove them away. Others feel that conquering tribes came from other countries and killed them.

Exercises

1. Answer the following.

(a) Why do we know more about the people of Egypt than about the people of the Indus Valley?

(b) What were the two main buildings found at Mohenjo Daro? What were they used for?

(c) What were the houses of the Indus Valley people made of?

(d) Describe the cities.

(e) What happened to the Indus Valley people?

(f) What do we come to know about the Indus Valley from the statues found there?

2. Fill in the blanks.

(a) The people of the Indus Valley built two famous cities at .... and ....

(b) They wrote on ....

(c) The roads of their cities were .... and ....

(d) The women kept ....

(e) In ...., some people working on railway tracks found some bricks which had been made by the stone masons of ....

Things to do

1. **Become an artist!**
   Try and make a seal with clay like the ones the Indus Valley people made. Draw designs on it with a matchstick. Let it dry. Display your seal in the class.

2. **Find the words.**
   In the box below, find seven words across or down connected to the Indus Valley Civilization. Circle the words.

H	G	R	E	A	T	B	A	T	H	S	I
A	H	J	W	V	F	N	R	R	N	B	N
R	G	R	A	N	A	R	Y	I	A	G	D
A	S	E	A	L	S	D	A	T	E	M	U
P	S	Y	O	T	D	R	H	W	B	V	S
P	M	Y	M	T	D	T	A	E	R	G	K
A	M	O	H	E	N	J	O	D	A	R	O
S	T	A	T	U	E	S	F	W	O	J	H

3. **Check out the following websites for more information.**
   http://www.harappa.com/har/moenO.html
   (accessed on 14 August 2006)
   http://www.bbc.co.uk/schools/indusvalley.html/
   ivl2_mdaro.shtml (accessed on 14 August 2006)

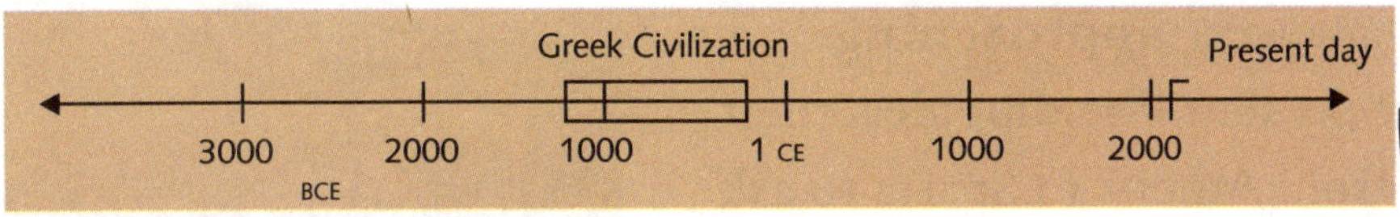

Greece

—The land of story-tellers

You have read about Egypt in Chapter 2. Now we are going to learn about another important country called Greece. Greece is in Europe and contributed greatly to the history of the world. About 4,000 years ago, people came from Central Europe to Greece. Greece is a country with many mountains and valleys. It was quite difficult for people to cross from one valley to another, and thus many small **states** grew up.

The city states were small. About 500 years before the birth of Christ they had to face a great attack from another country called Persia. The emperor of Persia was called Darius. The Greeks who joined together to fight Darius defeated him at a famous battle at Marathon. Marathon is a place about 40 kilometres from Athens (a powerful city state and now the capital of Greece).

Darius, the emperor of Persia

Words to remember

state : a large group of people living together and having a government and laws to control and guide them.

approaching : coming towards.

trapdoor : secret door, usually in the floor or the ceiling.

sacrifice : the killing of a person or animal as an offering to the gods.

When the Persians were **approaching** Athens, the Greeks sent Pheidippides, their fastest runner, from Athens to Sparta to ask for help. He ran as no man had ever run before. Not once did he stop to rest and he completed the 240 kilometres journey in 48 hours. He then ran back to Marathon and fought in the battle. After the battle Pheidippides ran to Athens to give the good news of victory to the people. As he reached the city and gave the good news, he fell dead. The Marathon race that we have today is a distance of 42 kilometres, and the name reminds us of that famous messenger of Greece.

Pheidippides

The battle of Marathon

The Greek city states

After the defeat of the Persians, Athens became the chief city in Greece. In fact it became the most important city in the world. Great men like Socrates, Plato, Aristotle and many other famous writers lived there.

Homer

The Greeks were fond of plays and story-telling, and one of the most famous Greek story-tellers was a man called Homer. Homer lived about 3,000 years ago and he wrote two famous poems, the *Iliad* and the *Odyssey*. Some people say that Homer was blind. When he sat down in the market-place all the people of the city would gather round him to listen. Most of the stories he told were about people who had lived long before him. Luckily Homer's stories were written down and we can still read them today.

Menelaus

Helen

The *Iliad* is the story of a great war between the Greeks and the Trojans. Menelaus, one of the kings of Greece, had a beautiful wife called Helen. She was carried away by Paris, the prince of Troy. The Greek kings got together a large number of ships, sailed across the seas, and attacked the city of Troy. Their attack lasted for ten years. Many battles were fought, many warriors were killed, but Troy could not be won.

In the Greek camp there was a wise man called Calchas. He called Odysseus (sometimes also called Ulysses), one of their brave soldiers, and all the other Greeks together and told them something useful.

'You must win the city of Troy by a trick,' he said. For a day or two, Odysseus thought about what the old man had said, and then he called everyone together. 'I have a plan," he said. 'We must build a huge wooden horse.')

Odysseus

His friends laughed loudly. 'What will happen?' they cried. 'Will the horse jump over the wall?'

'No, no!' cried Odysseus. 'Listen to me. We shall make a very big horse. It will be hollow inside and there will be a **trapdoor** so that our soldiers can get into it.'

His friends stopped laughing and began to listen. 'We shall make the horse so big,' continued Odysseus, 'that it won't go through the gates. When the horse is ready we shall put a hundred of our best soldiers into it and shut them in. One of us will remain here. We shall tie his hands behind his back and make his face dark with blood. The rest of us will get into our ships and sail away across the sea, leaving the horse and the man behind. We shall not go too far out to the sea; we shall go about seven miles so that the Trojans cannot see us. Then we shall wait.'

'What will happen then?' asked the others.

'I think this is what will happen,' said Odysseus. 'The Trojans will see our boats sailing away and think that we are going home. Then they will open the gates of Troy and find the man and the wooden horse. The man will tell them a story. He will say that we made the horse as an offering to the goddess Athene. He

Did you know?

The Greeks started the Olympic Games to honour their god Zeus.

will also say that he was captured by us and that we were going to kill him as a **sacrifice**. Then the Trojans would want to take the horse to the temple of Athene. It will be too big to get through the gates, so they will have to break the wall. When the horse is inside and everybody is asleep our man will open the trapdoor and our soldiers will come out. While they are killing the Trojans the man will light great fires on the wall which we can see from our ships. We can come back again then, and enter the city through the hole in the wall.'

'It is a fine plan,' said the Greeks.

They chose a man called Epeius to build the horse. He was the best carpenter in the army. There were many people to help and very soon the horse was ready. 'Now,' said Odysseus, 'we need brave warriors to get inside the horse and one man to act as the prisoner.' The door was opened in the horse and the bravest of the Greek heroes climbed up the ladder; the last man to get in was Epeius, as he had made the horse and knew how to shut the door.

A painting showing the Trojan horse being pulled into Troy

As soon as all the heroes were in the horse, the other Greeks set fire to their tents and sailed away in their boats. The horse and the prisoner remained outside the gates. Everything turned out just as Odysseus had planned.

The Trojans tried to take the horse into the city through the gates, but it was too big, and so they broke down a part of the wall. The prisoner was released and given a feast. The Trojans were happy because the Greeks had gone, and they too feasted and drank wine. After sunset when everyone was fast asleep, Epeius opened the door and all the warriors crept out quietly. They went from house to house killing the Trojans as fast as they could, and while they were doing this, the Greek prisoner started great fires on top of the walls. The Greeks returned in their ships. Troy was captured and Menelaus took Helen back to Greece with him.

Exercises

1. **Answer the following.**
   (a) Why were there a number of city states in Greece?
   (b) Who was the Greek messenger who ran from Athens to Sparta?
   (c) Why did the Greeks go to war with the Trojans?
   (d) Who told Odysseus that Troy should be captured by a trick?
   (e) Who made the wooden horse?

2. **Fill in the blanks.**
   (a) The Greeks joined together to fight ...., the king of the Persians.

(b) .... is a place 40 kilometres from Athens.

(c) The two long poems Homer wrote were the .... and the ....

(d) The Greek queen who was carried off to Troy was called ....

3. Say whether the following are True or False.

(a) It was easy for the people to cross the mountains and valleys.

(b) The Persians defeated the Greeks.

(c) Homer lived about 3,000 years ago.

(d) The Trojans were not able to take the horse into the city through the gates.

Things to do

1. For your scrapbook!

With the help of your teacher or parents find a picture of a Greek ship and paste it in your book.

2. Drawing activity.

Draw a picture of the wooden horse and colour it. Remember to show the trapdoor. You can take the help of the picture given.

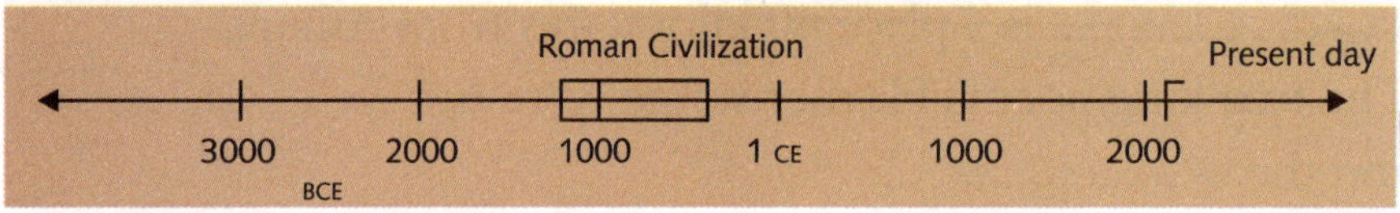

Romulus
—The man who built Rome

In the last chapter you learnt about the Trojan War which lasted for ten years. Finally the Greeks got into the city of Troy and destroyed it. One of the princes of Troy, a warrior called Aeneas, was able to escape from the city and sailed away towards Italy. He went around Sicily and landed on the coast of Italy at the mouth of the river Tiber. It was here that Aeneas's son built a city and called it Alba Longa.

Aeneas escaping from Troy

After many years a cruel man called Amulius made himself the ruler of Alba Longa by fighting against his brother, who was the king. The people of Alba

Words to remember

lair : a den or a cave where a wild animal lives.
site : a place chosen for building.
task : work that is to be done.
whirl : to move quickly round and round.

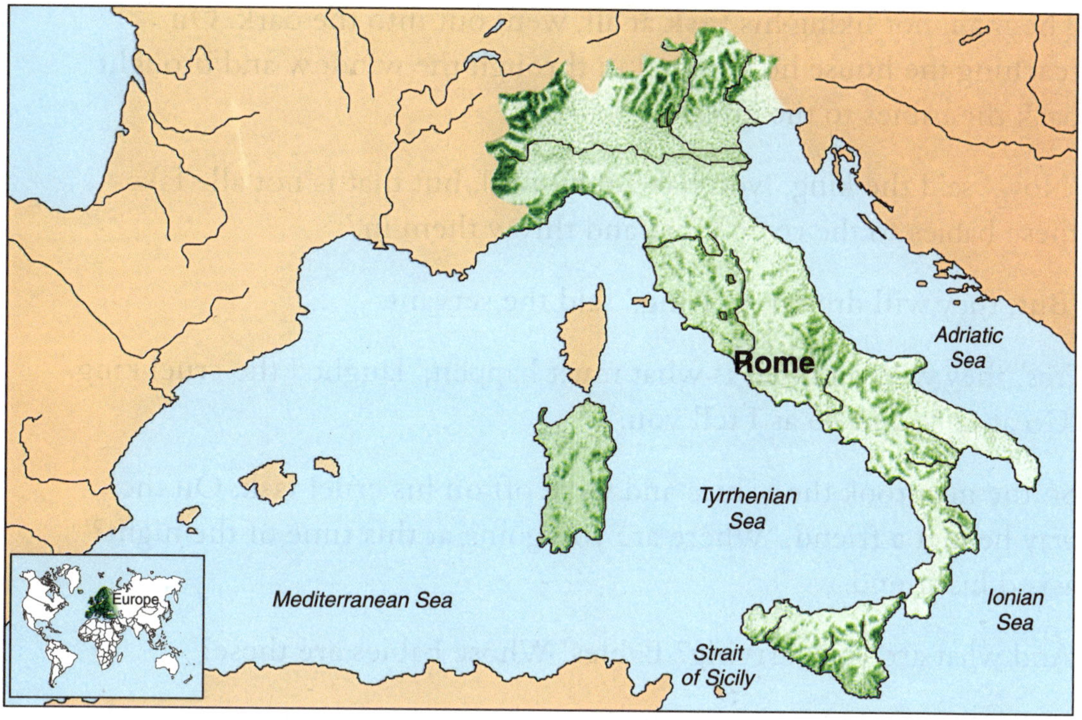

Longa disliked him, but did not do anything because they were afraid to attack him. Amulius was very pleased with himself as he knew how powerful he was. However, one day when he heard that his brother's daughter had given birth to twin boys he was both angry and afraid.

'When they grow up,' he said to himself, 'they will attack me and take away my throne. I must get rid of them.' He called one of his servants, who came and bowed low before him.

'Go to my brother's house,' commanded the king. 'There you will find that his daughter has had two baby boys. Wait until it is dark and then go quietly into the house and bring the babies to me.'

'But, O King...' began the man.

'Do you dare to question me?' shouted the king. 'You know what I will do to you if you disobey me; go at once and bring me the babies.'

The man, not liking his **task** at all, went out into the dark. On reaching the house he climbed in through the window and brought back the babies to the king.

'Now,' said the king, 'you have done well, but that is not all. Take these babies to the river Tiber and throw them in.'

'But, they will drown, O King,' said the servant.

'Yes, they will, and that is what must happen,' laughed the cruel king. 'Go at once and do as I tell you.'

So the man took the babies and went off on his cruel task. On the way he met a friend. 'Where are you going at this time of the night?' asked his friend.

'And what are you carrying? Babies! Whose babies are these?'

The servant told him about the king's plan to drown the babies. 'You are not going to throw those little babies in the Tiber, are you?' asked his friend.

'It will break my heart,' said the man, 'but if I take back the babies to the king he will surely throw me to the lions. He will then kill the babies himself, so they will die in any case.'

His friend thought for a minute and then said, 'I have a plan. In my house I have a large basket. Let us put the two babies in the basket and float it down the Tiber. Someone will find it, and look after the babies. You can go back to the king and tell him the truth, that you put the babies in the Tiber.'

Romulus and Remus in the basket

The servant did just as his friend had said. He then returned to the palace and told the king that he had done his work.

The basket **whirled** and twirled down the river until it rested against an old tree trunk which had fallen half into the water. The basket stuck fast against the tree trunk, and the babies slept peacefully. The next morning when they woke up they started crying. There was no one about in that lonely place except an old she-wolf. Mother Wolf was sad that morning, because she had lost her cubs the night before. When she heard the cries of the babies, she carefully looked though the bushes and saw them lying in the basket. She watched them for a minute or two and then went closer. The babies felt a warm body near them and thought it was their mother. They reached out their hands towards the wolf and the old wolf licked them. Then she took up the babies carefully one by one and took them to her **lair**.

The mother wolf

So the boys were taken care of by the Mother Wolf for a week or two. One day a shepherd was passing that way and saw the smiling baby boys. When he saw that there was no one around he picked them up and took them home to his wife. His wife was very happy, because they had no children. They named the boys Romulus and Remus and brought them up as their own sons.

The wolf looked after the babies

Romulus and Remus grew up and became clever boys. They soon became leaders of the village and people listened to what they said. King Amulius seemed to become more cruel every day. Romulus and Remus led the people against him and killed him.

A painting showing the shepherd looking at the babies

They then decided to leave the village and build a city. 'Where shall it be?' asked Remus.

'Why, near the river Tiber,' said Romulus.

When they got to the river Tiber, however, they found seven hills.

'We should build the city on this hill,' said Romulus.

'No, no,' cried Remus. 'This hill is much better. Let us build the city here.'

They fought over this the whole day, until in the evening Romulus said, 'Since we cannot decide where to build the city, let the gods decide.'

'How will the gods decide?' asked Remus.

'They will show us a sign.'

So Romulus and Remus each stood on the hill he had chosen. Each had his friends with him.

They looked up towards heaven. Very early in the morning Remus saw six birds flying across the sky.

'There,' he cried, 'look at the birds, six of them! It is a sign from the gods; we should build the city on my hill.'

But just at that moment, Romulus saw twelve great vultures flying across the sky.

'Look,' he shouted, 'twelve vultures! Twice as many as your birds! That means we should build the city on my hill.'

Romulus looking at the sky

Did you know?

The children in ancient Rome went to school and learnt music, history, geography, public speaking and literature!

And Romulus built the city and called it Rome after his own name.

Years later the city spread to cover all the seven hills and that is why Rome is also called 'the city of the seven hills'. Later on Rome became the capital of the Roman Empire. Today it is the capital of Italy, a country in Europe.

Exercises

1. Answer the following.

(a) Why was King Amulius worried when he heard that his brother's daughter had given birth to twin boys?

(b) What did he ask his servant to do?

(c) What did the babies do when they saw the Mother Wolf ?

(d) What did the boys become when they grew up?

(e) Who built the city in the end? Why?

2. **Choose the correct word from among those given in brackets.**
   (a) The servant .... (obeyed/disobeyed) the king.
   (b) Remus and Romulus were .... (twins/brothers)
   (c) The boys were put into a .... (box/basket)
   (d) Remus saw six .... (vultures/birds)

3. **Fill in the blanks.**
   (a) .... was a Trojan prince who escaped and sailed to ....
   (b) His son built a city there called ....
   (c) Another name for Rome is the ....
   (d) Today Rome is the capital of ....

Things to do

1. **Unscramble the jumbled words.**
   (a) BRITE ....
   (b) BAAL GOLAN ....
   (c) ASEAEN ....
   (d) THMOER LOWF ....

2. **Find the meanings.**
   There are many sayings about Rome. Given below are two very common ones.
   (a) All roads lead to Rome.
   (b) Rome was not built in a day.
   With the help of your teacher find out their meanings and use each one of them in a sentence.

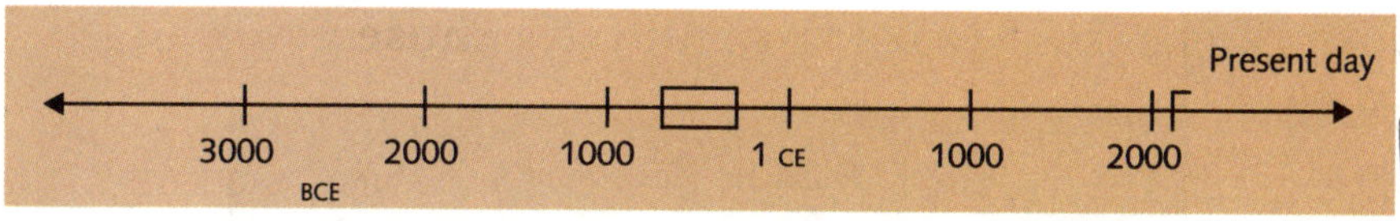

China
—The land of Confucius

China today is a very large country and, like Egypt, it has a very important river flowing through it, called the Hwang Ho. The name means Yellow River, because it carries yellow soil with it. Each year, when it rains, the river carries down soil to the plains in the north of China. The land is very flat and when the river is full it floods the flat land. When the rain stops, and the river gets smaller, the soil is left on the plains. Many thousands of years ago the Chinese discovered that this soil was very fertile and good crops would grow in it.

It was difficult for people to live there because every year the floods came and carried away their houses. The Chinese had to work very hard. They made ditches and they put up **dykes** to stop their houses from being carried away. Even though the river brought them fertile soil they called it 'the river of sorrow'.

Words to remember

dykes : stone or mud walls made to stop flooding.

criminals : those who break the laws of the state or country.

official : one who holds an office or an important job.

introduced : brought something into.

Around 550 BCE (that is, just over 2,500 years ago) there lived a famous teacher in China. His name was Confucius. His teachings are famous throughout the world. His father was an **official** in the small state of Lu. Confucius' father was very poor, because he had lost some of his land in the tribal wars. Confucius was only three when his father died and as soon as he was a little older he had to earn his living. But he also learnt to read and write. He was a very clever boy and when he grew older he started teaching other students. He got married and then got a job. He was in charge of the parks in the state. He became a small official like his father.

Confucius

Confucius soon saw that people were unhappy. The traders in the state were dishonest and cheated the poor families who came to buy things from them. The rich people disobeyed the laws of the land as and when they liked. Confucius was interested in teaching people to lead a better life. Young men came to him to learn and he started a small school. At the same time Confucius carried on with his work as an official. He was honest and good at his work.

Did you know?

Tea was discovered in China about 4,500 hundred years ago. It is believed that Emperor Shen Nung was boiling drinking water and a few leaves of a wild tea tree blew into the water. He realized that the leaves gave a special taste and flavour to the water and so it became his favourite drink!

A painting showing Confucius writing a book

When he was 52 years old the Chief of Lu made him the Chief Justice of the state. **Criminals** who came before him were judged wisely, and soon his name became famous. He was later made the Prime Minister of Lu. He looked after the poor and fixed the prices of the things in the shops. This made it difficult for the rich traders to cheat the poor farmers. They became angry with Confucius and after a few years he had to leave the state of Lu. His name was still well known, however, and he travelled all over North China. While he travelled he taught, and he always had a number of students with him.

A temple built in memory of Confucius in Southern China

Confucius taught people how to lead good lives. He taught people that everyone should do one's duty as well as one could. He laid down rules for husbands and wives, fathers and children. He was a wise and great teacher and his teachings are read even today.

Did you know?

The Chinese were the first to breed silkworms and make silk cloth. The road on which this silk was taken to other countries came to be known as the Silk Route.

China at that time was full of tribes, and these tribes were always fighting one another. Each king wanted to own more and more land. At last one state conquered all the others. This was called the state of Ch'in, and the name China comes from this word.

Huang Ti

About 300 years after Confucius lived, a famous Emperor called Huang Ti ruled over the state of Ch'in. When Huang Ti came to the throne there were still many small states. He conquered all these states. He **introduced** a number of changes. Until then all the states had used different kinds of money. Huang Ti made everyone use the same money. Huang Ti was also interested in writing. People at that time had been writing for many hundreds of years. Each state had a different way of writing. Huang Ti made everybody write in the same way. This meant that people from one part of the country could read the writing of other parts of the country.

There were still many enemies of China, especially in the north. Many tribes used to come into China from the north. As they entered the villages they set fire to the houses and took away everything they could find. Huang Ti sent his soldiers everywhere, but the robber tribes continued to attack. At last Huang Ti decided to build a wall to stop them from coming in easily. This is called the Great Wall of China.

Any map of China would show it going right across China from the east coast to the Gobi desert. It is about 2,400 kilometres long, and six meters high, and on top of the wall there is a road which can be used by carts. There are also many towers on the wall. These towers were

The Great Wall of China

built so that Huang Ti's soldiers could stay in them and fight the tribes when they came on their horses. At some places there are gates in the wall, to allow people to pass through to the mountains or to the Gobi desert. Each gate has wooden doors; the front of the door is studded with great nails, and it is locked at night. The wall goes on and on like a great snake across the countryside, it goes up over the mountains and across the valleys and rivers. Initially the wall was made of stones and earth but later on bricks and well-cut stones were used.

The Great Wall of China is there even today, and traffic still passes through the gates—camels and donkeys, mules and herds of sheep. Nowadays, there are trucks and lorries, cars and motor cycles, too. But they still follow the same routes into China that were used 2,000 years ago.

Exercises

1. **Answer the following.**
   (a) Why did the Chinese people build dykes?
   (b) Why were the Chinese people unhappy?
   (c) What did Confucius teach?
   (d) Besides building the Great Wall, what else did Huang Ti do for China?

2. **Fill in the blanks.**
   (a) The river in China which brings yellow soil to the plains is called the ....
   (b) Confucius was born in China in the state of ....
   (c) Confucius taught people to lead good ....
   (d) China got its name from the state called ....
   (e) The Great Wall of China was built by ....

Things to do

1. **For your scrapbook!**
   Find samples of Chinese writing or pictures of Chinese people and stick them in your book.

2. **Make a lantern for Chinese New Year!**
   You need: Coloured paper (construction paper or gift wrapping); scissors; glue, tape or a stapler.

- Fold a rectangular piece of paper in half, making a long, thin rectangle.

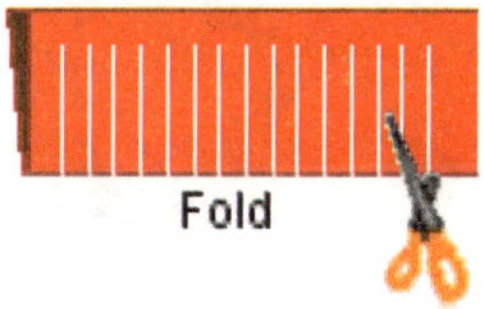

- Make a series of cuts (about a dozen or more) along the fold line. Don't cut all the way to the edge of the paper.

- Unfold the paper. Glue or staple the short edges of the paper together.

- Cut a strip of paper 6 inches long and 1/2 inch wide. Glue or staple this strip of paper across one end of the lantern — this will be the handle of the lantern.

- Make a lot of lanterns and string them along a length of string. Decorate your classroom!

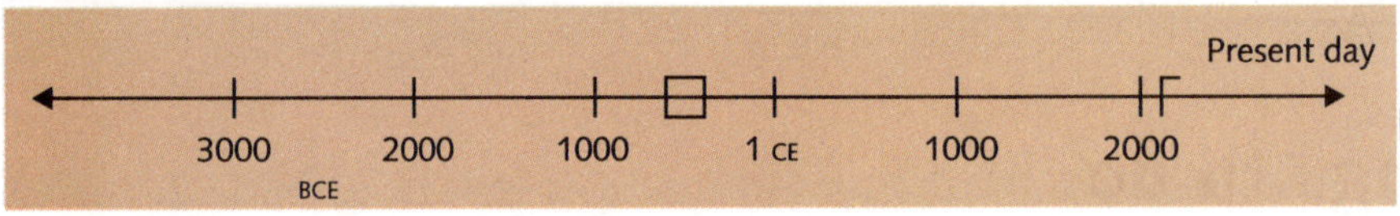

The Buddha

—The enlightened one

Nearly 2,500 years ago there lived one of the greatest men the world has ever known. His name was Gautama. His mother Mayadevi died soon after he was born. His father Suddhodana was the ruler of a small kingdom near Nepal called Kapilavastu. When Gautama was born, wise men from far and near came to see the baby. 'He has the marks of greatness,' they cried, 'and will one day rule the world, but only if he remains at home. If he ever leaves home he will become the Buddha, which means the **Enlightened One**.'

The birth of Buddha

Words to remember

enlightened : wise.
chariot : horse-drawn car used in ancient days.
wandering : journey from place to place, often with no particular purpose.
preaching : making a religion or belief known by talking about it publicly.

Gautama was not only handsome but

very clever too. As a prince he had rich clothes to wear, good food to eat and a big palace to live in. He was taught how to ride a horse, how to shoot and how to swim; in fact he learnt all that a prince should know. Gautama was very good at his lessons as well and so his teachers were pleased with him. But Gautama was not a very happy boy. His father did not allow him to leave the palace because he was worried that his son might leave home to become a **wandering** holy man. He did not enjoy playing games with other children and could not laugh and sing with them. He would go in the garden all by himself and sit quietly. He would spend a lot of time thinking about the things around him.

Young Prince Gautama

When Gautama was nineteen years old, his father got him married to a princess called Yashodhara. Gautama and Yashodhara were both very happy and lived in a lovely palace. After some time a son was born to them and they named him Rahula.

One day Gautama went out driving in his **chariot**. His chariot driver went with him. On the way they saw an old man leaning on a stick and walking along. Gautama stopped the chariot and got down, for he had never seen an old man.

'Who is this?' asked Gautama.

'He is a man,' said his chariot driver.

'But I am a man,' said Gautama, 'and I am not like this.'

'Yes,' said the chariot driver, 'you will be. But come sir, leave this old man by the side of the road. Let us go back to the palace and not worry about this.' But Gautama kept on thinking!

Some days later, Gautama went out again and this time he saw a sick old man. This made him even more sad. 'The body grows old', he said to himself, 'but does it get sick too? Is there nothing in life greater than our bodies?'

Weeks went by and Gautama longed to go out in his chariot again. He sent for his chariot driver and away they went. While they were driving through the city, Gautama saw a dead body being carried by some people. 'Is there nothing which will last forever?' he asked. 'No,' said the chariot driver, 'everything must die.'

Finally Gautama went out for the fourth time and saw a man dressed in simple clothes; his head was shaven.

The four sights troubled him

'Who is he and why does he look so peaceful and happy?' asked the prince.

'He is a holy man who has given up everything,' replied the chariot driver.

'Strange,' said the prince; he has nothing and yet looks so happy,' and once again he began to think.

Gautama thought about this for many weeks and at last he decided to leave the palace and go out into the world. One evening he went to bed as usual, but in the middle of the night he woke up. Everything was quiet and still. When he looked out of the window he saw the moon shining down on the palace gardens.

'Now is the time,' he said to himself, 'now is the time to leave.'

He looked down sadly at his wife and his son fast asleep. Then he got up and walked out of the palace. For many years he studied with different teachers, but he was never satisfied. 'We do not find truth in sadness,' he said, 'nor in riches nor in pleasure nor in pain.'

He left his teachers and walked along the dusty road towards a place called Gaya. By the side of the road he found a *pipal* tree. He sat down in the shade of the tree and started to think. He thought about the poor and the rich, the old and the sick. He thought about the priests and the teachers, the temples and the prayers to the gods. He remained under the tree all day and night. At last he found the Truth—to bring happiness to all humans while they lived on the

The first sermon

earth. That one day and night under the *pipal* tree had changed him. From then on he was called not Gautama, but the Buddha, which means 'the Enlightened One'. The tree under which he sat came to be known as the Bodhi tree.

Did you know?

Lord Buddha taught people to follow the eight fold path or the middle path—a life that was not too comfortable or too difficult.

Lord Buddha believed in non violence or ahimsa. He wanted everyone to live in peace and wanted people to be kind to everyone.

Once Lord Buddha was walking down the road followed by several disciples. Seeing him, his jealous cousin Devadatta let loose a drunken elephant hoping that it would trample the Buddha to death.

Buddha and the elephant

As the angry elephant charged down the street people ran everywhere. The followers of Buddha begged their master to flee. The Buddha, however, remained calm and refused to run away. The elephant came charging straight at him.

The Buddha calmly raised his hand in a gesture of non-violence. The angry beast stopped dead in its tracks! It then humbly kneeled down before the Buddha. Such was the power of Lord Buddha's non-violence.

The Buddha thought that the way to bring happiness to all humans was to get them to follow certain rules; to tell the truth, not to harm

A statue of Buddha from Sarnath

other people and to think rightly. He travelled all over the country **preaching** these simple things. He had many friends who believed in what he taught. Just before he died he told them, 'When I am not here, Truth shall be your teacher.'

The teachings of the Buddha have spread all over the world and the religion he started is called Buddhism. Although he lived so many years ago, we still remember him as one of the greatest teachers of the world.

Exercises

1. Answer the following.

(a) What does 'Buddha' mean?
(b) What did the Buddha teach?
(c) What is his religion known as?
(d) Name the 'four sights' that made Gautama think even more deeply.

2. Fill in the blanks.

(a) Gautama's father .... was the ruler of ....
(b) His mother .... died soon after he was born.
(c) Gautama learnt how to .... and shoot.
(d) He could .... as well. He was a .... boy and did his lessons well.

3. **Say whether the following are True or False.**
   (a) Gautama did not play like the other children.
   (b) Lord Buddha was able to stop the charge of the mad elephant.
   (c) Buddha got enlightened under a banyan tree.
   (d) When he was twenty five his father got him married.

Things to do

1. **For your scrapbook.**
   Try and find a picture of the Buddha. Paste it in your book.

2. **Find a story!**
   The stories and lessons of the Buddha's life are known collectively as the *Jataka Tales*. Try and find one story from the *Jataka Tales* and read it out in class.

Unit Test 1

Maximum Marks: 15

1. Give one word for the following. **½×6=3**

(a) The study of things, buildings and monuments that people have left behind.

(b) The name given to the Egyptian king

(c) The remains of old cities and buildings

(d) A large group of people living together and having a government

(e) Making a religion or belief known by talking about it publicly

(f) A famous symbol of the Egyptian civilization

2. Answer the following. **1×6=6**

(a) What is history?

(b) Why do we know less about the Indus Valley Civilization than the Egyptian Civilization?

(c) Name the Greek messenger who ran from Athens to Sparta.

(d) Who found the basket in which Romulus and Remus had been left?

(e) Why was the Great Wall of China built?

(f) What were the four sights that disturbed Gautama?

3. Fill in the blanks. **½×8=4**

(a) Paper was invented in ....

(b) ....was the name of the Egyptian sun god.

(c) The ....was the most important building in Mohenjo Daro.

(d) Homer wrote .... and............

(e) ....ruled over the state of Ch'in.

(f) The tree under which Buddha sat is known as the .... tree.

(g) The people of the .... wrote on seals.

4. On an outline map of the world mark the following. **½×4=2**

(a) River Nile (b) Mohenjo Daro (c) Athens (d) Rome

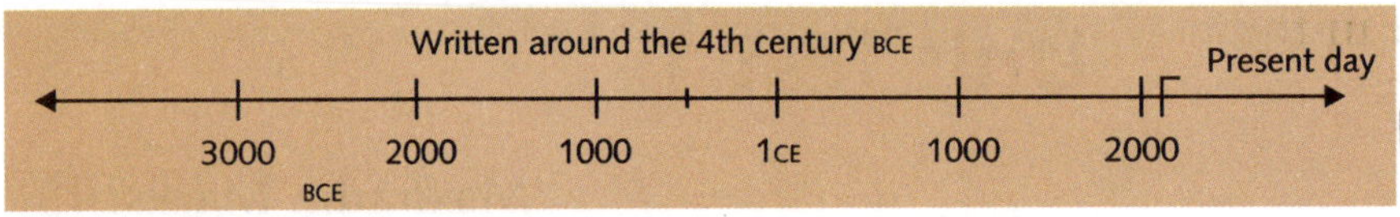

The *Ramayana*

—The victory of good over evil

You must have heard of the *Ramayana*. It is a very old poem or epic written by **sage** Valmiki, and like the *Mahabharata*, it is full of exciting stories.

King Dasharatha was the ruler of Ayodhya. He had four sons. Rama was the eldest and would have become king after his father. But his stepmother Kaikeyi wanted her own son Bharata to be the next king. So she made king Dasharatha send Rama and his wife Sita out of the kingdom to live in the forest. Lakshmana, who loved his brother Rama dearly, went along with them.

Sage Valmiki

Rama, Sita and Lakshmana wandered for a long time in the forest. They moved from one place to another and survived on what

Words to remember

sage : wise and holy man.
general : head of the army.
herb : a plant used for making medicines.
rescue : to save somebody from a harmful situation.

they could find in the forests. One day they left Sita alone and went off in search of food. While they were away, the king of the demons or rakshasas, the ten-headed Ravana, tricked Sita and carried her off to Lanka. When Rama and Lakshmana returned, they were very sad to find that Sita was not at home. They searched for her everywhere but could not find Sita. At last, Sugriva, the king of the monkeys, and Hanuman, one of his **generals**, came to Rama and promised to find Sita.

Rama, Sita and Lakshmana leaving for the forest

Ravana in disguise with Sita

Sugriva, Hanuman, and the other monkeys searched for Sita everywhere but could not find her. At last Hanuman found Sita sitting in a garden in Ravana's palace. She was a prisoner there

Did you know?

The *Ramayana* is composed of verses or paragraphs called *shlokas*, in the Sanskrit language.

and Hanuman brought back the news to Rama.

Hanuman promised to find Sita

Ravana heard about the search for Sita. He was very angry. He did not want to lose Sita. His brother Vibhishana asked him to let Sita go back to Rama or else face a big battle in which they would surely lose. But Ravana refused. So Vibhishana left him and went to Rama, who was happy to see him. But the monkeys who had seen Vibhishana in Lanka were afraid and cried out to Rama, 'Do not believe him, O Rama! He will play some trick on us.' But Rama believed Vibhishana and promised to make him the king of Lanka after he had killed Ravana.

Rama, Lakshmana, Vibhishana, Sugriva, Hanuman and a large band of monkeys now moved towards Lanka to **rescue** Sita. A bridge had to be built across the sea and so all the monkeys worked very hard. They collected rocks and stones and branches of trees and soon the bridge was ready for them to cross into Lanka.

Making the bridge

In Lanka the two armies fought day and night. Many lay wounded and many others died. Lakshmana too was badly wounded and could only be saved by the magic **herbs** found on the high Himalayas. Hanuman agreed to go and fetch them.

Up on the Himalayas, Hanuman searched for the magic herbs and not being sure about which one to take, he carried the whole mountain on his hand to Lanka. And thus Lakshmana was saved.

Hanuman carried the whole mountain

Day after day the battle went on, till one morning sage Agastya came to Rama. 'O Rama,' he said, 'now is the time to say your prayers to the sun god, the Lord of the whole world. He will help you to conquer Ravana.' Rama prayed to the sun god and then went in search of Ravana.

The battle

Did you know?

The story of the *Ramayana* travelled to many countries of South East Asia. In Thailand the *Ramayana* is known as the *Ramakien* whereas in Kampuchea it is called *Reamker*.

When Rama saw Ravana he shot him in the head with his bow and arrow. He shot many arrows and each arrow cut off one of Ravana's ten heads; but as one head was cut off, another head grew in its place. At last Rama used the magic arrow that Agastya had given him and shot Ravana dead.

Rama and Sita then returned to their kingdom leaving Vibhishana as the king of Lanka. All this while, Bharata had looked after the kingdom for Rama. He was happy to see his elder brother back on the throne as the king.

Exercises

1. **Answer the following.**
   (a) How many sons did King Dasharatha have?
   (b) Where did Ravana take Sita?
   (c) Who helped Rama to build the bridge?
   (d) What advice did Vibhishana give Ravana?

2. **Fill in the blanks.**
   (a) Kaikeyi wanted .... to be King.
   (b) Vibhishana was Ravana's ....
   (c) A .... had to be built across the sea to cross into Lanka.
   (d) Lakshmana could only be saved by magic .... found on the ....
   (e) The sage who told Rama to say prayers to the Sun God was called ....

3. **Match the following.**

(a) Sugriva	A wise sage
(b) Vibhishana	Carried the mountain
(c) Hanuman	Brother of Ravana
(d) Agastya	The king of monkeys

Things to do

1. **Try to find these stories:**
   (a) How Ravana tricked Rama and took Sita away.
   (b) How Rama won Sita in marriage.
   (c) How Rama met Hanuman.

2. **Find and circle the following words in the puzzle below.**

AGASTYA	BHARATA	HANUMAN	SITA
RAMA	LAKSHMANA	SUGRIVA	VIBHISHANA

A	J	H	W	F	A	V	A	L	V
G	B	H	A	R	A	T	A	A	I
A	F	A	I	N	A	F	B	K	B
S	C	S	M	R	U	H	F	S	H
T	F	I	T	A	A	M	T	H	I
Y	A	T	V	M	S	X	A	M	S
A	A	A	H	A	W	K	A	A	H
H	A	N	U	M	A	N	A	N	A
B	N	C	B	O	P	O	E	A	N
A	S	U	G	R	I	V	A	Q	A

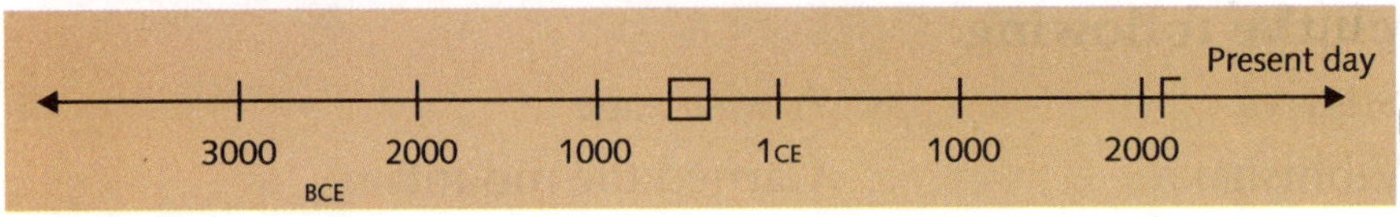

Socrates

—A great and wise man

About 2,500 years ago there lived a stone-cutter in Athens, in Greece. He had a son named Socrates. In those days, Athens was a very famous and important city. There was a large market-place and there were many beautiful gardens. The water for the city was brought from a nearby river. There was a great theatre where the people of Athens could watch plays and there was a **stadium** where games were played.

A stone statue of Socrates

Words to remember

stadium : an area of land with a wall around it used for games, etc. usually with stands for the spectators.

government : a group of people who work together for the good of the country. They make laws.

arrested : to take and keep prisoner under law.

assembly : a place where people meet together.

honour : respect

Socrates grew up in Athens and learnt the art of stone-cutting from his father. The people of Athens wanted to build new buildings and so there was always plenty of work for Socrates. While Socrates was learning how to cut stone, he was also going to school. At school he learnt how to read and write and he made many friends. When he grew up and left school he joined the army. He spent four or five years in the army and fought in many wars. But he was not like other soldiers. In the evening, when the day's march was over, Socrates would sit with his friends round the camp-fire and ask them questions. He was always trying to find out what was the right thing to do. He wanted to know the truth about everything.

A picture showing how a theatre would have looked in ancient times in Athens

When Socrates left the army he went back to Athens and continued to help his father. Athens was growing bigger and many new buildings were being made. Socrates cut and carved stones for buildings during the day, but in the evenings after his work he went to the market-place. He sat there with his friends and

Did you know?

Athens was a beautiful city with many buildings and temples. The Parthenon was a great temple built for goddess Athena, the protector of the city. Athens is named after her.

talked. They talked about the **government** of Athens, about religion and the gods. Socrates was always curious to find out the truth about these things. He wanted to know how humans could lead a good life and be happy without hurting one another.

Socrates made many friends and he talked to many people. Unfortunately, some important people in the government did not like Socrates because he asked too many questions. They **arrested** him and put him in the prison. They said he would be tried before the judges in the Assembly.

A painting showing Socrates in discussion with friends

When the day of the trial came, Socrates was taken from the prison to the **Assembly**. The Assembly was full; everybody in Athens wanted to hear the trial. A large number of citizens made speeches blaming Socrates for ruining the character of the people in the city. They said he did not believe in the Greek gods and told lies to the young men of the city. They also accused Socrates of making young people ask too many questions. At last their speeches were over and Socrates was asked to reply.

'None of you like the truth,' said Socrates. 'You cannot kill me nor can the judges. Truth will kill me, because everybody dislikes it. I am not afraid of death. Even if you let me out of the prison I shall go on trying to find the truth, and I shall go on telling people to ask questions.'

The court did not like this at all and they ordered that Socrates should be put to death. He was sent back to the prison once again.

After he had been in prison for about three weeks, some friends came to visit him.

'We shall get you out of the prison,' they said, 'we shall give the guard some money and he will open the door in the middle of the night. You can easily escape. Everything has been arranged.'

'Why should I escape from this prison?' asked Socrates. 'You will be free,' said his friends. 'You can go on asking questions. The people who ordered that you should die are evil. We must fight them.'

Socrates with the cup of poison

'You told me that you would give some money to the guard so that he would let me out,' said Socrates, 'but that would not be right. To live is nothing; to live rightly is everything. You also said that the people who have ordered me to be put to death are evil. Never give evil for evil. Evil cannot come from a good man. For these reasons I cannot agree with your plan. Have you anything to say?'

'We have nothing to say,' said his friends, but their eyes were filled with tears.

A little later the prison guard came and gave Socrates a cup of poison. 'Can I pour out a little in **honour** of the gods?' asked Socrates.

'No,' said the guard. 'There is only enough for you. You must drink it all and walk about until your legs become heavy.'

'Then at least I can offer a prayer to the gods for a safe journey. I do not know where the journey will end, but perhaps the gods will look after me.' With this he began to say his prayer.

When he had finished his prayers he drank the poison from the cup. His friends began to weep, but Socrates asked them to stop. He walked about until his legs became heavy; then he lay down and the poison slowly reached his heart. His body became cold and his friends covered him with a cloth. After a little while he shut his eyes and died. That was the end of a great and wise man.

Exercises

1. Answer the following.

(a) Who was Socrates and how many years ago did he live?
(b) Why was there always plenty of work for Socrates when he was young?
(c) In what way was Socrates different from the other soldiers?
(d) Why was Socrates arrested?
(e) What was Socrates accused of at the trial?
(f) How did his friends plan to get him out of the prison?
(g) Why did Socrates not agree to his friends' plan?

2. Choose the correct word.

(a) The water for the city of Athens came from a nearby river/lake.
(b) There was a stadium/theatre where the people of Athens watched plays.
(c) Socrates learnt the art of carpentry/stone-cutting from his father.

(d) The prison guard gave Socrates a cup of water/poison.

3. **Fill in the blanks.**
   (a) After school Socrates joined the ....
   (b) Socrates wanted to find the ....
   (c) People in the government did not like Socrates because he asked ....
   (d) The judges called Socrates to the .... to try him.
   (e) Socrates was in prison for .... weeks.

Things to do

1. **Become a potter!**
   The Greeks were famous for their pottery. Given alongside is an example. Try and copy the pot in your notebook. Colour it.

2. **Check these websites for some interesting information.**
   http://www.bbc.co.uk/schools/ancientgreece
   (accessed on 11 August 2006)
   http://www.historyforkids.org/learn/greeks/art/greekart.html
   (accessed on 14 August 2006)

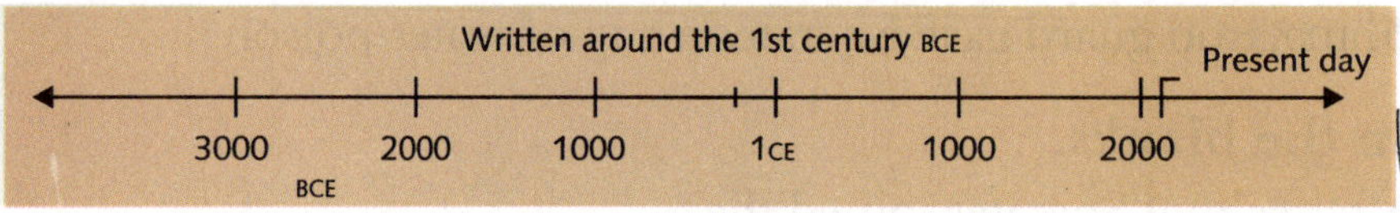

The *Mahabharata I*

—The dice game

The *Mahabharata* was written more than 2,000 years ago by Vyasa. It is a very long poem and has about two hundred thousand lines. Although the main story is about the Kauravas and their cousins, the Pandavas, there are also many other wonderful stories about kings and princes and gods and demons. There is also a famous passage called the *Bhagavad Gita* or the Song of the Lord, about which you may have heard earlier.

Sage Vyasa

Words to remember

dice : a small cube of wood, bone etc. marked with spots for 1 to 6. (The singular is *die*, but commonly we use only the plural, *dice*.)

persuade : make someone do or believe something.

challenge : call someone to fight or play a game.

stake : money and other things risked in a bet.

hesitated : paused uncertainly.

protest : object to something.

kshatriya : a member of the warrior class.

disguise : a thing worn or used to make somebody/something look or sound different from the usual.

Many years ago, in the city of Hastinapur in northern India, there lived a king who had three sons. The eldest son was blind and he was called Dhritarashtra. The second son was called Pandu and the third son was Vidura. Dhritarashtra had a hundred sons, who were called the Kauravas, while Pandu had only five sons, who were called Pandavas. Yudhishthira was the eldest son of Pandu, and Duryodhana the eldest son of Dhritarashtra. The Kauravas were afraid that Yudhishthira would be made the king as all the people liked him; so they decided to kill all the Pandavas. One day as Duryodhana was sitting in his palace thinking of how to get rid of the Pandavas, his uncle Shakuni came into the room.

The court of Dhritarashtra

'Are you thinking about the Pandavas?' asked Shakuni.

'Yes, I am,' said Duryodhana. 'They must be destroyed.'

'I have a good plan,' said Shakuni, 'You know that Yudhishthira is fond of playing **dice**. We shall invite him to come here to the palace. You can challenge him to a game of dice and win everything he has. We can then make the Pandavas do as we like.'

'But what will happen if I lose?' asked Duryodhana.

'I shall play for you,' replied Shakuni. 'I am better at dice than you are and know how to cheat if necessary.'

Duryodhana carried out his plan very carefully. A beautiful palace was built and when everything was ready, he sent some friends to challenge Yudhishthira to a game of dice.

The Pandavas knew how much Yudhishthira liked dice and were afraid that he would lose everything. They knew that Duryodhana was clever and cunning and that he wanted to harm them. So they tried to **persuade** Yudhishthira not to accept the **challenge**.

'Do you think I am a coward?' cried Yudhishthira. 'Do you think I am afraid of Duryodhana? He has **challenged** me and I shall accept the challenge.'

When they got to the palace, Duryodhana was waiting for them with Shakuni at his side.

'Come,' he cried, 'sit down and play. Are you afraid to play?'

'I am not afraid,' cried Yudhishthira, 'and you will soon see that I can play with dice as well as I can fight on the battlefield. Come, let us start.'

Yudhishthira threw down his gold necklace as a **stake** for the first game. Duryodhana took off his gold necklace and put it on the board beside the first one. Shakuni leaned over and took up the dice for the first throw.

'What's this?' cried Yudhishthira. 'I came to play you Duryodhana, not your uncle.'

'What does it matter?' said Duryodhana quietly. 'He will play for me. Are you afraid? If you are, say so and we shall stop the game.'

Yudhishthira **hesitated** for a moment and then he banged the board with his first.

'No,' he cried, 'I am not afraid. Throw the dice.' Shakuni threw the dice on the board, and then it was Yudhishthira's turn—he lost.

'What does it matter?' thought Yudhishthira to himself. 'This is only the first throw. I shall easily win back the gold necklace and much more besides.'

A painting showing the game of dice

But he did not. He went on losing more and more. He lost his necklaces, he lost all his treasure and his gold and silver jewels. He lost his chariots, his elephants and his horses. He lost all his servants. But still he continued to play. He staked his kingdom and he lost that too. At last he had nothing left.

His brothers came to him and begged him to stop.

'You will lose your life,' they cried.

But Yudhishthira was so excited that when he saw his brothers he cried out with a loud voice, 'Now the stake in the game will be Nakula, my brother!' All the people watching the match tried to stop him, but he was too excited to be stopped.

'Throw the dice, throw the dice!' he shouted. 'Nakula is the stake!'

And he lost again. Then one by one he staked all his brothers. At each throw Shakuni won and at last Yudhishthira stood alone.

'Enough, enough!' cried the people sitting round. 'You are penniless. You have lost your kingdom, you have even made your brothers slaves.'

The Duryodhana bent across the board and whispered in Yudhishthira's ear, 'Don't forget your wife, the beautiful Draupadi; she is still there; perhaps she will bring you luck and you will win back all that you have lost.'

'I stake Draupadi!' shouted Yudhishthira, and all the onlookers were surprised and angry.

'Go,' cried Duryodhana, 'bring her here!'

In spite of all her **protests**, Draupadi was dragged to the hall. Dushshasana, Duryodhana's brother, dragged her to the hall by her hair.

Draupadi praying to Lord Krishna

The dice was thrown and once more Yudhishthira lost, and Draupadi belonged to Duryodhana.

Duryodhana was delighted with his revenge. He had won everything that Yudhishthira had, including his brothers and his wife. Although people asked him to be kind to Yudhishthira, he refused. However, when he left the hall King Dhritarashtra who was ashamed of his son, tried to persuade Draupadi not to be angry. She stood before Dhritarashtra, a brave and proud woman, and asked him to release Yudhishthira.

'I grant your wish, my child,' he said. 'You may have another wish and yet another.'

Then Draupadi asked for the freedom of all the brothers.

'You have another wish,' cried Dhritarashtra. 'Ask for the return of your husband's kingdom and his treasure.'

Did you know?

The *Mahabharata* is the longest epic in the world consisting of eighteen books!

'That I will not do,' said Draupadi. 'A **kshatriya** is allowed only two wishes. However, now that Yudhishthira and his brothers are free, I am not worried as they can conquer the whole world.'

And so they left. When Duryodhana returned, he was mad with anger. He decided to call back the Pandavas for another game. This time it was agreed that whoever lost the game would go into the forest for twelve years. In the thirteenth year he would have to live in the world in **disguise**, but if he were recognised he would have to go back into the forest for another twelve years.

In spite of his brother's protests, Yudhishthira came back to play the final game and lost again. So the Pandavas, along with Draupadi, their wife, went into the forest, where they remained for twelve years.

Exercises

1. **Answer the following.**
   (a) Why did Duryodhana want to get rid of the Pandavas?
   (b) What was Shakuni's plan?
   (c) What was the first thing they used as a stake?
   (d) What were the two wishes that Draupadi asked for?
   (e) What happened in the final game?

2. **Fill in the blanks.**
   (a) Dhritarashtra had .... sons, called
   ....; Pandu had .... sons, called
   ....

(b) Duryodhana invited Yudhishthira to play a game of ....

(c) .... played instead of Duryodhana.

(d) The Pandavas had to stay in the forest for .... years.

(e) The Pandavas had to remain in disguise for .... year.

3. **Write a sentence about each of the following.**
Yudhishthira, Duryodhana, Dhritarashtra, Nakula, Draupadi.

Things to do

1. **For your scrapbook!**
Find a picture of a palace and paste it in your scrapbook.

2. **Find a story!**
The *Mahabharata* is full of stories. Try and find any of the following:
(a) Eklavya, the great archer
(b) The lac palace
(c) The vessel that was never empty

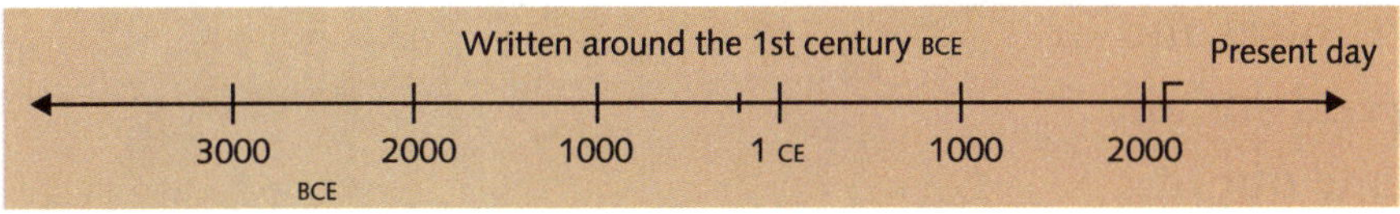

The *Mahabharata II*

—The great battle

Yudhishthira, his wife Draupadi, and his brothers had to go into the forest, where they wandered for twelve years. In the thirteenth year they came out of their **exile** and decided to serve the king of Virata. They were careful and disguised themselves because they knew that if they were recognized they would have to spend another twelve years in the forest.

Did you know?

Yudhishthira was disguised as a travelling musician and Bhima as a cook. Arjuna was in disguise as a lady dancing teacher, Nakula and Sahadeva were dressed up as cowherds and Draupadi was a lady-in-waiting and hairdresser to the queen.

Words to remember

exile : to send someone out of one's country as punishment.
orphans : children whose parents are dead.
coward : a person who is not brave.
mace : a thick wooden stick with a heavy spiked metal head.

After many adventures the year came to an end and the five brothers came out of their hiding. They wanted to get back their kingdom and knew that they would have to fight many battles. Both the Pandavas and the Kauravas began to gather their friends around them and get ready for a great war. Both sides went to Krishna, who was their cousin. Both the sides valued his advice. They asked for his help. He said that he would join one side and tell them what to do. To the other side, he would give a large army. They were free to choose what they wanted. Yudhishthira chose Krishna and Duryodhana chose the large army. Krishna agreed to act as the chariot driver of his friend Arjuna.

Duryodhana and Yudhishthira with Krishna

The two armies faced each other at a place called Kurukshetra. The battle went on for many days, until most of Duryodhana's brothers had been killed. Bhima, the strongest of the Pandavas, killed most of the remaining brothers, until there were only four people left.

The two armies get ready for battle

An illustration of the battle from an old book

In the end Duryodhana ran away from the battlefield. He ran as fast as he could but the Pandavas followed him. At last, very tired after all the fighting, he rested in the long grass near a lake.

The Pandavas soon found his hiding place. They too were very tired after the battle. But they wanted to take their revenge on Duryodhana because they could not forget the way he had treated Draupadi.

'Come out,' they cried. 'Are you a **coward**? You were brave when you beat Yudhishthira at dice; where is your bravery now?'

Duryodhana cried out, 'These days of battle have tired me. My brothers and my friends have all been killed. My kingdom is full of dead bodies and **orphans** and widows. You may take it, Yudhishthira. Take it and rule it. It is yours.' Yudhishthira laughed.

Did you know?

The *Bhagavad Gita* is an important part of the *Mahabharata*. It contains seven hundred verses. It is a dialogue between Arjuna and Lord Krishna.

'After all these years of fighting you want to give me your kingdom. We do not need your presents! Why should we accept a gift from you, when we can take the kingdom for ourselves? Come out and fight!'

The dialogue between Lord Krishna and Arjuna

'You are five and I am one,' cried Duryodhana. 'What kind of a fight is that?'

'Come out,' cried Yudhishthira. 'We will fight you one at a time. You shall choose who you want to fight first.'

At last Duryodhana came out of his hiding place and said that he would fight Bhima.

And so they fought. They fought with **maces** as big as tree trunks. Although Duryodhana was very tired he was a good fighter. He pushed Bhima back step by step, striking him on the shoulder again and again with his heavy mace. The Pandavas looked on. They were afraid that Duryodhana might kill their strongest warrior. At last Bhima lifted his mace high above his head, and with one blow smashed Duryodhana's thigh.

Duryodhana and Bhima

Duryodhana fell and Bhima danced with joy. The battle of Kurukshetra was over. The Pandavas had won. Yudhishthira was crowned the king. The Pandavas resumed their princely duties.

Exercises

1. **Answer the following.**
   (a) Why did the Pandavas disguise themselves?
   (b) Why did Duryodhana hide in the long grass?
   (c) Why did the Pandavas want to take revenge on Duryodhana?
   (d) When did Duryodhana come out of his hiding place?
   (e) How did the great battle end?

2. **Fill in the blanks.**
   (a) The Pandavas came out of their exile and served ....
   (b) The battlefield where the Kauravas and the Pandavas fought was called ....
   (c) Yudhishthira chose .... to help him.
   (d) Bhima struck Duryodhana on the ....
   (e) Duryodhana and Bhima fought with .... and not with swords.

Things to do

1. **For your scrapbook!**
   Look for a picture of Krishna in his chariot. Paste it in your scrapbook.

2. Complete the puzzle!

Across

5. The place where the battle took place
7. An important part of the *Mahabharata*
8. The chariot driver of Arjuna

Down

1. The wife of the Pandavas
2. He wrote the *Mahabharata*
3. He ran away from the battlefield
4. The strongest of the Pandavas
6. The number of years the Pandavas were in exile

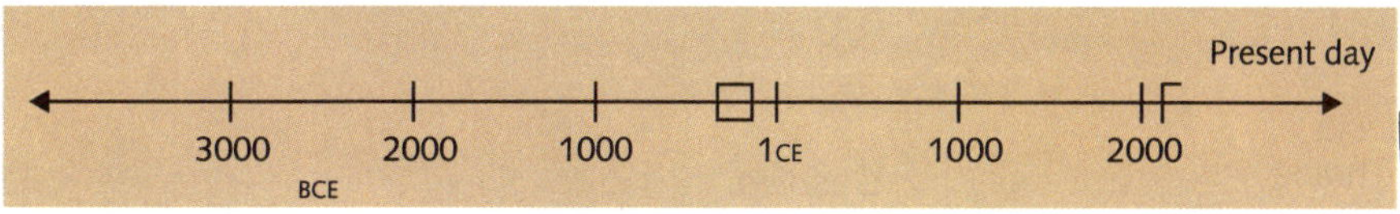

Alexander

—The great conquerer

Alexander was one of the greatest generals in history. He was the son of king Philip and queen Olympias of Macedonia in Greece. You can locate Macedonia in the map on the next page.

Queen Olympias

King Philip

Alexander was brought up in Macedonia, and as a prince he learnt not only reading, writing, and science from his teacher Aristotle, but also how to ride and shoot. His father wanted him to be a soldier when he grew up. Alexander was a very good rider. One day he went with his father to a great horse fair. He watched beautiful horses walking up and down as their master showed them to the people who

Words to remember

mane : the long hair on the back of a horse's neck.
archers : people who shoot with bows and arrows.
generous : ready to give freely.
courage : bravery.
invasion : attacking and entering a country or city.
trampled : stamped underfoot.

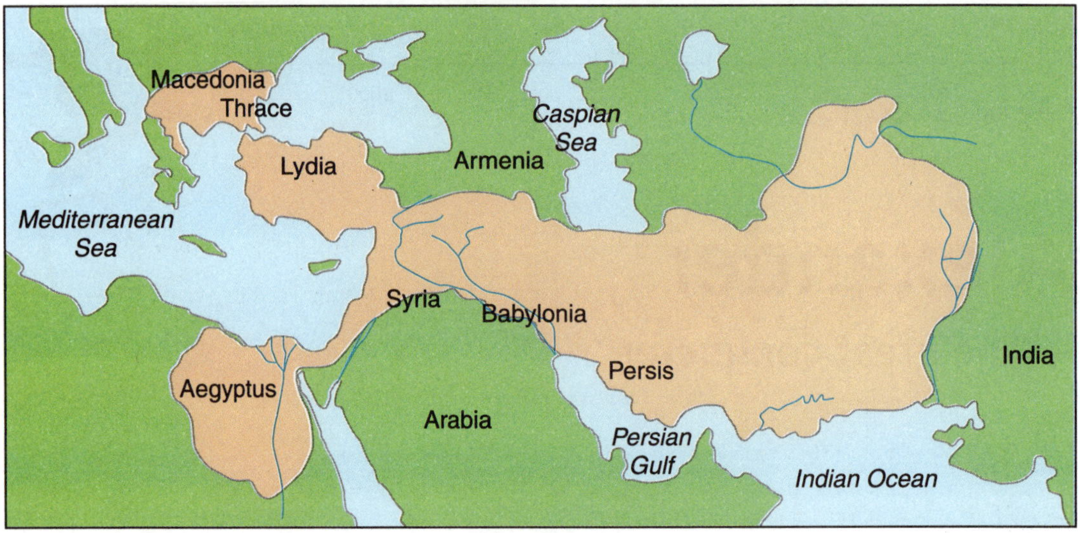

Alexander's Empire

Alexander the Great

wanted to buy them. Suddenly his eyes fell on a fine young horse standing in a corner. He had a white star on his forehead and looked frightened. Every time someone went near the horse, he would put his ears back, and kick his legs up in the air. 'That is a fine horse,' said Alexander to his father. 'That is the horse I would like; he is brave and strong.'

'He looks dangerous, too,' said King Philip. 'I don't think you can ride him.'

'I am sure I can, father,' said young Alexander. 'The horse is not dangerous. He is frightened. Every time he looks down and sees his shadow, he jumps up in the air.'

'May I try and ride him, father?' he asked.

King Philip laughed and said, 'If you can ride that horse, my boy, I shall buy it for you.'

Alexander went forward slowly and stood with his back to the sun. He made a soft noise in his throat and the horse turned towards him. Alexander moved to one side of the horse and the horse looked down. He could not see his shadow and so he remained quiet. Alexander slid gently on to the horse's back, took his **mane** between his hands and trotted slowly across the fair ground. Alexander named the horse Bucephalus and kept him for many years.

Alexander and Bucephalus

When Alexander was a young man his father died. King Philip had conquered all the Greek states, but Alexander was not content with only Greece as his kingdom. He wanted to conquer the whole world. Alexander was a fine soldier besides being clever and brave. He first led his armies into Egypt and conquered it. After Egypt, he moved across to Persia.

Darius, king of Persia

The Persians were good fighters and had fine horsemen and **archers**, but most of their foot–soldiers were countrymen from the hills. Darius, the king of Persia, tried to save his country. He crossed over to eastern Persia and tried to collect some troops. Alexander and his men followed as fast as they could; they marched for thirty-six hours without stopping. They did not have to go very far because they found Darius lying on the sand; he had been stabbed to death by his own men.

Alexander was not only a good soldier but a good ruler as well. He tried to give justice to all. He was also very **generous**. He gave a great deal of treasure to his old teacher, Aristotle. When the army was not fighting, he kept the soldiers busy with several competitions, at which rich prizes were given to the winners.

Alexander in battle

Sometimes Alexander came across people who were as brave as he was. Once a man who had stolen a sheep was brought before him. When Alexander asked him why he should not be put to death, the thief stepped forward bravely and said:

'You can kill hundreds of men all over the world and take their treasures, jewels, gold and silver. For this, people call you a great man and give you their blessings. Yet when I take one sheep, you call me a thief and condemn me to die.'

Alexander was pleased with the man's **courage** and let him go.

Did you know?

Alexander took Callisthenes, a Greek historian, along with him on his Asiatic expedition. Callisthenes recorded the happenings during his travels.

After Alexander had conquered Persia, he decided to come to India. The Persians, too, had come to India before him but had remained only in the north. Alexander had heard that the Indians were very good fighters, so he made great preparations for the **invasion**. He brought in many new archers and made some of his best soldiers Captains. He sent many of his old and tired soldiers back to Greece and took new soldiers from Persia.

In 326 BCE, Alexander entered India through the Hindu Kush mountains. He crossed the Indus River and entered the kingdom of Taxila where Ambhi was the ruler. Ambhi was happy to see Alexander and treated him well. He even helped Alexander by giving him soldiers and elephants. Ambhi wanted Alexander to fight against his enemy Paurava, another Indian king, who had his kingdom next to his. The Greeks called Paurava, Porus.

Porus was a brave king and would not give in to Alexander without a fight. The two stood on opposite banks of the river Jhelum. The monsoon had just started and Alexander knew that he could not cross the river where Porus could see him. He sent his scouts up and down the river to find a place from where he could cross the river Jhelum. His efforts were soon rewarded. On a dark and cloudy night, Alexander moved his army sixteen miles up the river from where he could easily cross the river into the kingdom of Porus.

Porus and Alexander

A fierce battle was fought. Porus did not expect the attack at night but his men fought every bravely. There were arrows and spears everywhere, and wounded elephants **trampled** the soldiers to death. At last Alexander and his men won the battle. Porus was wounded and captured. He was brought before Alexander.

'Aha,' cried Alexander, 'you have been wounded and the battle is over. You have lost and now your kingdom belongs to me. What should I do with you, now that you are my prisoner?'

'Treat me like a king,' replied the brave Porus. Alexander was pleased with his answer and gave back Porus most of the kingdom he had lost.

Alexander wanted to conquer other kingdoms in India too, but his soldiers were tired and wanted to go back to their homes. Alexander decided to go back. He sent half his army by sea and the other half he took with him along the coast. In 323 BC he reached Babylon, where he died. He was only 33 years old at the time of his death.

Did you know?

Alexander did not lose a single battle his entire life!

Exercises

1. Answer the following.

(a) Why was Alexander not afraid of the horse?
(b) What did Alexander want to do?
(c) How did Porus want to be treated?
(d) Where did Alexander die?

2. **Match the following.**

(a) Philip	An Indian king
(b) Bucephalus	King of Persia
(c) Porus	Alexander's horse
(d) Darius	King of Macedonia

3. **Say whether the following are True or False.**
   (a) Plato was asked to teach Alexander.
   (b) Ambhi, the ruler of Taxila, did not treat Alexander well.
   (c) Alexander gave back Porus most of the kingdom he had lost.
   (d) Darius was killed by his own soldiers.

Things to do

1. **Find out!**
   Just like Alexander had a favourite horse, one of our Indian kings had a favourite horse called Chetak. Find out the name of the king, where he ruled and some stories about him.

2. **Check out the following website for some interesting information.**
   http://www.bbc.co.uk/history/historic_figures/alexander-the-great.shtml (accessed on 11 August 2006)

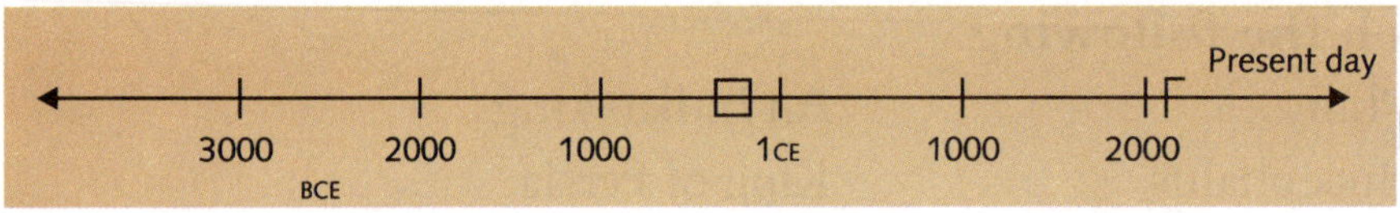

Ashoka

—The king who gave up war

After Alexander left India, a family of kings, the Mauryas, began to extend their rule over the country. The first king was Chandragupta Maurya. Chandragupta left his kingdom to his son Bindusara, who ruled for 25 years. In about 272 BCE Bindusara's son Ashoka came to the throne. Ashoka became a high official while his father was still alive. He ruled over Kashmir and Punjab, and later over the western part of India where there was a famous city called Takshashila, which is now known as Taxila. When he came to the throne, he was already an **experienced** ruler.

Ashoka built a great empire. He conquered a large part of India, but he was unable to conquer one part of the country in the east, between the Mahanadi and the Krishna rivers. This was the area belonging to people called the Kalingas.

Words to remember

experienced : one who has learnt by doing and seeing things.

reign : period of rule.

strainer : cloth or net used to keep water clean. Water is poured through it and all the dirty things in the water stick to the strainer while the clean water comes through.

missionaries : people sent out to preach a religion.

order : a group of priests.

edict : an order or official statement issued by an authority.

Ashoka's empire

About nine years after he came to the throne, Ashoka sent his armies to attack the Kalingas. The Kalingas, who had so valiantly resisted Chandragupta Maurya, could no longer defend their country. Ashoka's armies proved too strong for them. Many thousands of Kalingas were killed on the battlefield. Ashoka's army swept through the country, burning villages and killing everyone they could see.

Ashoka won the country of the Kalingas. When the war was over, Ashoka looked around him and saw the suffering the war had caused.

The battle of Kalinga

He saw thousands of dead and wounded soldiers. He saw their wives and children weeping. It is said that he was so disturbed by this sight that he vowed never to fight a battle again. He changed his name from Ashoka to Priyadarsin. He adopted Buddhism, which believed in non-violence. Ashoka wanted everyone to live in peace. He also wrote his feelings about the Kalingas on a rock-face. It says this:

'His majesty, King Priyadarsin, has conquered the Kalingas in the ninth year of his reign.'

'150,000 prisoners were carried away, 100,000 were killed there, and many more died.'

Ashoka was the first king who had ever given up war.

Did you know?

Ashoka wanted his people to live happily. He appointed special officers who travelled all over the country and talked to people to find out if they had any problems.

For some years Ashoka lived a very simple life. He carried with him only eight things, which the Buddhist rule allowed. They were three pieces of orange cloth, to cover his body; a belt to hold it together; a needle to mend it; a razor to shave his head; a **strainer** to make sure that no living beings fell into his drinking water; and a bowl to beg for his food.

Ashoka ruled his kingdom wisely. He put up many fine buildings, and travelled all over the country preaching the teaching of the Buddha. He asked people to be kind to one another and to tell the truth; he asked them not to kill any living beings. In addition, he had pillars and **edicts** put up all over the country on which he wrote his teachings. He sent his preachers all over the country, to southern India, to the western coast, to the Himalayas and even to Ceylon (Sri Lanka). His **missionaries** not only carried the teachings of the Buddha to Sri Lanka, they also carried a branch of the sacred bodhi tree from Bodh Gaya. It was under this tree that Gautama became the Buddha.

An Ashokan edict

An old sculpture of Ashoka in Sri Lanka

The emperor did many other things

Did you know?

The pillars and edicts were placed in public places so that everyone could read them. They were mostly written in the Prakrit language using the Brahmi script. The most famous pillar is the pillar with the four lions. It is our National Emblem.

apart from teaching the word of the Buddha. He made many gardens and stone arches. He planted trees along all the main roads in the country so that the travellers had shade to rest. He dug wells in many places. He gave medicines and money to the poor.

The stupa at Sanchi

He also put up many buildings called **stupas**. A stupa was a building meant to hold some remains of the Buddha or of a saint. Sometimes they were built in honour of the dead. The most famous of these stupas is at Sanchi.

Ashoka was truly a great king and richly deserves the title of 'the great'. He died around 232 BCE and the Mauryan dynasty declined soon after.

Exercises

1. **Answer the following.**
   (a) Why did Ashoka give up fighting wars?
   (b) What did Ashoka do for the spread of Buddhism?

(c) Name the eight things that Ashoka carried with him.
(d) Why did Ashoka plant trees?

2. Fill in the blanks.

(a) Ashoka was the son of ....
(b) Ashoka gave up fighting wars after conquering the ....
(c) Ashoka sent a branch of the .... tree from Bodh Gaya.
(d) The most famous stupa is at ....

3. Say whether the following are True or False.

(a) Ashoka was the first king of the famous Mauryan family.
(b) The people of Kalinga lost the war.
(c) Ashoka was the first great king who gave up war.
(d) Ashoka wanted his people to be happy and live in peace.

Things to do

1. Discuss in class.

Ashoka is known as 'Ashoka the great'. Can you say why?

2. Find out!

This is a picture of our National Emblem. Think and write where and on what you have seen this emblem.

The lion capital

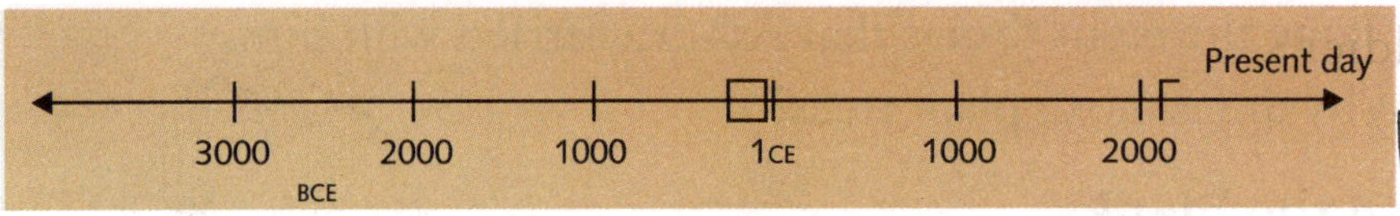

Hannibal

—The man who crossed the Alps

On the north coast of Africa there was a city called Carthage and the people living there were called the Carthaginians. Soon the Carthaginians became as powerful as the Romans. Between Carthage and Rome was the island of Sicily which was a very important city for trade. See the map on page 94. Both the Carthaginians and the Romans wanted to control it. So they both began preparations for a war to control Sicily.

The chief of the Carthaginian army was a man called Hamilcar. Hamilcar was a great soldier and his men liked him. He had a young son called Hannibal. Hannibal spent all his time in the soldier's camps. He played with their spears and sometimes pretended to fight like a soldier. Hannibal did not like toys or games that other boys played. He learnt to run and to fight. He was always fighting with the other boys in the camp. Like his father and the other Carthaginians, he disliked the Romans.

Words to remember

cavalry : a group of soldiers who fight on horseback.
might : strength; great power.
trotted : ran with short steps.
gasped : caught one's breath in great surprise.

'I shall be a soldier soon,' he used to say to his friends, 'and I shall drive the Romans out of Italy.'

Hannibal

His friends laughed. 'Your father, who is such a famous general, cannot do that. How do you think you can?' they said.

'I shall also be a famous general,' he said. 'Just wait and see!'

When he grew up to be a young man, Hannibal joined the army and fought many battles. He was a fine soldier and after a few years he became a general like his father. He sailed across the Mediterranean Sea in the Carthaginian ships and fought against the Romans in Sicily but he could not capture the island.

One night he sat thinking in his tent. 'There must be some way of beating the Romans,' he said to himself. 'But whenever we go to Sicily we always lose.'

He thought for a long time and at last he got an idea. In the morning he called all his officers.

'We shall set sail next week,' he cried. 'Get everything ready. We are going to Spain. See that all our soldiers are ready to go on board. We shall take our elephants, **cavalry** and foot-soldiers.'

'Why are we going to Spain, General?' asked one of the officers.

'We shall pass through Spain, and then we shall turn eastwards to attack Rome from the north,' replied Hannibal.

'But we will have to cross over two great mountain ranges, the Pyrenees between Spain and France, and the snow-covered Alps between France and Italy. How will our soldiers, horses and elephants cross these mountains?' asked another officer.

Hannibal's army on the way to Rome

'With courage, my friend,' said the general, 'Let everything be ready.'

So they sailed to Spain and marched through it. Later they crossed the Pyrenees. Then they turned eastwards, and at last they came to the Alps.

The route Hannibal followed

This was the most difficult part of the journey as winter had set in. The mountains were high, and covered with snow. Snow fell thickly as the huge army pushed further and further up the Alps. They climbed for days. Every evening they put up their tents and cooked their food. The officers then met Hannibal in his tent and told him the news of the day. Every day it was sad news.

'We have lost three elephants, and more than five hundred men have died of cold,' said one officer.

'This morning a great block of snow came sliding down from the mountains and carried off more than two hundred of our men,' said another.

'Forty horses died today,' said the third.

Hannibal lost most of his army during the journey

Every day there were losses, but Hannibal kept on encouraging his men. He too suffered with them. At last the remaining elephants, horsemen and foot-soldiers arrived on top of the Alps and as they looked down they could see the plains of Italy. This gave them new hope.

After resting for a day or two they started on their way down. When they reached the plains, Hannibal had only a few elephants left. More than half of his army had died on the way and those that were left were tired and sick. However, when they entered Italy they attacked

Roman soldiers in the battle of Zama

the Romans with all their **might**. Hannibal went over Italy in all directions and won many battles. Hannibal's stay in Italy ended when he was called back to Africa to save Carthage. Carthage was attacked by the Roman army under a famous general called Scipio. At last, in a great battle at Zama, Scipio defeated Hannibal.

Hannibal and a few officers managed to escape. A band of Roman horsemen followed them. Hannibal and his officers hid in an old farmhouse. It was still very cold but they were afraid to light a fire because the smoke would be seen by the Roman soldiers.

Ruins of Carthage

'They may not look for us here,' said one of the officers. 'They may think that no one lives here.' Suddenly he **gasped**. From the window he had seen the helmets of the Roman soldiers as they **trotted** up to the farmhouse. They could hear them coming closer and then came the loud knocks on the door.

'Open the door in the name of Rome,' cried a voice. 'We know you are inside.' The officers looked towards Hannibal for his orders, but they saw Hannibal lying on the floor, dead. When one of his officers turned the body over he noticed a ring on Hannibal's finger. Hannibal had a tiny box of poison in his ring and when they saw it open, one of them cried out, 'He has poisoned himself. He preferred to die than be a prisoner,' said another. And then the Romans broke down the door and rushed into the room.

Exercises

1. **Answer the following.**
   (a) Why were the Carthaginians and Romans fighting?
   (b) What did Hannibal desire to be when he grew up?
   (c) What difficulties did Hannibal and his army face while crossing the Alps?
   (d) Why did Hannibal poison himself?

2. **Fill in the blanks.**
   (a) The .... built a great city called Carthage.
   (b) The chief general of the Carthaginians was called ....
   (c) Hannibal led his army through .... and climbed the .... and the .... to attack Italy from the north.
   (d) Hannibal was defeated by a famous Roman general called ....

Things to do

1. **Solve the puzzle!**
   Complete the puzzle with the help of clues given below.

Across

2. The battle in which Hannibal was defeated
4. The island for which they fought

Down

1. Hannibal's father
3. Hannibal crossed these mountains
4. A famous Roman general

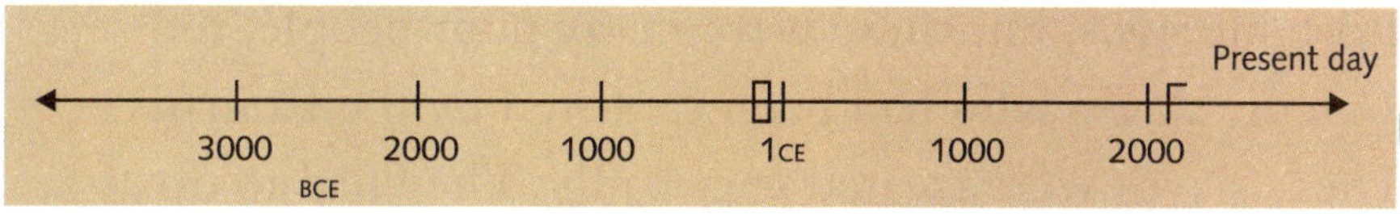

Julius Caesar

— The famous Roman General

In the story of Romulus and Remus you have read how Rome was founded. At first the city of Rome was surrounded by enemies, but it had able rulers and slowly the enemies were beaten back. One of these rulers was a king called Tarquin. Tarquin was so cruel and wicked that the people of Rome fought against him and drove him out of Rome. They decided that they would have no more kings, but choose two of their wisest men to be their leaders or **consuls**.

Rome was a big city and there were more than a million people in it in the great days of the Roman empire. There were fine buildings, theatres, and stadiums. The rich

Rome had many beautiful buildings

Words to remember

consuls : two men who were chosen by the people every year to govern Rome.

dictator : a ruler who has total power over his country.

senate : a meeting of men who made laws and governed Rome. They were mostly chosen from among the Roman nobles.

stabbed : wounded with a dagger.

people led comfortable lives, but there were many poor people, too. There were also many slaves who had been captured by the Romans in the battles. These slaves were treated very badly. They had to do whatever work they were given and were never paid for it. Many of the slaves had to fight with hungry lions or big bulls so that the rich could have their fun.

Julius Caesar was born in Rome in 100 BCE. Though he was not a very strong boy, he always wanted to be the greatest man of Rome when he grew up. For this he knew he had to win the hearts of the common people. He was a very good speaker and could inspire people with his speeches. He spent a lot of money on people by arranging free entertainment for them and very soon everybody knew and liked him. He was made the governor of Spain and then of Gaul, which is now called France. He was also one of the two consuls who ruled Rome.

A statue of Julius Caesar

Pompey

At that time there was another general called Pompey. He was popular with the people and also a good general, too. He married Caesar's daughter and they were good friends. Caesar knew that if they stayed in Gaul, Pompey would become more powerful than he was. He wrote to the officers of the government (**senate**) at Rome and asked them to let him come back. But the generals in Rome knew that Caesar with his large army was a danger to them.

'You can come to Rome,' they wrote, 'But it is better if you leave your army in Gaul.'

Caesar with his army

Julius Caesar was very angry at this and decided to take his army with him. The boundary of Gaul was marked by a river called the Rubicon. When Caesar came to this river on his way to Rome, he stopped and called his generals together.

'This river,' he said, 'is our boundary line. The Romans have told me not to cross it with my army, but I am going to cross it.'

Crossing the Rubicon

'Crossing the Rubicon' is now a well-known saying; it means taking a step or doing something from which there is no turning back. Caesar did not turn back either. He marched on to Rome with his army behind him and beat Pompey in three battles. When he reached Rome, the people were very happy to see him. They made him the **dictator** of the country, and they put up a statue in his honour.

Julius Caesar soon became so powerful that many people in Rome became jealous of him. He had many enemies, and these enemies joined together and decided to kill him on 15 March. On the morning of 15 March, Caesar was getting ready to go to the senate as usual. His wife came out of her room and said, 'My Lord, I beg you not to go to the senate today.'

'I have some important business there. Why should I not go?' asked Caesar.

'I have had a bad dream,' replied his wife. 'A dream!' cried Caesar. 'What has that got to do with the senate?'

'I dreamt that men were killing you. They had daggers in their hands and they plunged these daggers into your heart.' 'It was only a nightmare,' said Caesar. 'Go to your room and rest. Nothing will happen to me. I shall go to the senate.'

'No, no!' cried his wife. 'I beg you not to go! I saw them killing you.'

Did you know?

Julius Caesar made a new Roman calendar. The month in which he was born was named July after him.

A painting showing the enemies of Caesar about to kill him

Caesar laughed again. 'I have work to do,' he said, 'I cannot stay at home because of a dream. What will people say? They will laugh at me and say, 'See! Caesar's wife has had a dream and so he is afraid to come to the senate!' His wife began to cry, but he refused to listen to her and went to the senate.

But the murderers were waiting for him. As he stood by the side of the statute of Pompey, his old enemy, they pounced on him and **stabbed** him to death.

Exercises

1. **Answer the following.**
   (a) Why did the Romans decide to have no more kings?
   (b) How did Julius Caesar try to become the greatest man in Rome?
   (c) Why did some of the important people of Rome want to kill Caesar?

2. **Fill in the blanks.**
   (a) The cruel king who ruled Rome was called ....
   (b) The two new rulers of Rome were called ....
   (c) Caesar crossed the .... when he left Gaul and began to march towards Rome.
   (d) Pompey married Caesar's ....

Things to do

1. **Design a coin.**
   Given alongside is a picture of a coin showing an elephant crushing a snake, and the name Caesar on it. It was meant to show Caesar crushing his enemies. Can you design a coin that shows what you would like to do or become when you grow older?

2. **Find out!**
   Some months of our calendar are named after historical personalities or gods and goddesses. Find out about these months.

Unit Test 2

Maximum Marks: 15

1. **Give one word for the following.** **½×6=3**
   (a) A wise and holy man
   (b) People sent out to preach a religion
   (c) A group of soldiers who fight on horseback
   (d) A ruler who has total power over his country
   (e) To send someone out of one's own country as punishment
   (f) A group of priests

2. **Answer the following.** **1×6=6**
   (a) Where did Ravana take Sita?
   (b) Why was Socrates arrested?
   (c) Why did Duryodhana want to get rid of the Pandavas?
   (d) How did Porus want to be treated?
   (e) Why did Alexander return home from the border of India?
   (f) Name any three things that Ashoka did to make the lives of his people easier and happier.

3. **Fill in the blanks.** **½×6=3**
   (a) .... ruled over Ayodhya.
   (b) The Carthaginians and the Romans wanted to control the island of ....
   (c) The Romans chose two of their wisest men to be their ....
   (d) The boundary of .... was marked by the river Rubicon.
   (e) Ashoka wrote his teachings on ....
   (f) Alexander entered India through the .... mountains.

4. **Say whether the following are True or False.** **½×6=3**
   (a) Yudhishthira chose the army and Duryodhana chose Lord Krishna.
   (b) Socrates lived in Rome.
   (c) Sage Agastya had given Lord Rama a magic arrow.
   (d) Hannibal was captured by the Romans.
   (e) Julius Caesar's wife warned him to be careful.
   (f) The Pandavas had to be in disguise for twelve years.